Life Out
Loud

Hi Doug !
you inspired
this authorship ?

Life Out Loud

A Memoir of Countless
Adventures and No Regrets

Ed Nef

The Ed Nef Foundation
601 North Fairfax Street, Unit 507
Alexandria, VA 22314

Printed in the United States of America

First Printing, 2020

ISBN print: 978-1-7341716-0-0
ISBN e-book: 978-1-7341716-1-7

Library of Congress Control Number: 2019919042

Frontispiece and background painting of Mongolian landscape by Ed Nef. All photographs come from the author's personal collection.

Book design by K. M. Weber, www.ilibribookdesign.com

Dedicated to my family—wife Elizabeth and three daughters Christine, Patricia, and Stefanie, who have made my life so much more fun and interesting, and who constantly contribute to the good humor, serious dedication, and positive attitudes we all share.

———————————

Contents

I Quit the Government and Began the Happiest Years of My Life

For me, the half-century marked the beginning of the best years of my life. Passing away were the self-doubts, the incertitude of the future, the worries of "What is going to happen next?" By then I knew myself better and had gone through all the doubts and fears. Don't like your boss? He doesn't like you? Screw him. You don't need him and can do better without him. Before fifty, I was still scared.

Half a career in the Foreign Service had passed with not much to show—just plodding up the career ladder. Increasingly, I wondered if the Foreign Service was for me. Just as I was hoping to be promoted as a political officer in Guatemala, the State Department decided that they really needed—and would henceforth promote—administrative officers. Not so important were those of us who had labored to get to know the country of assignment, analyze its relations with the US, and suggest courses of action to protect and promote US interests.

So I did not get promoted—a big disappointment to me and my supervisors. My tour ended and I was transferred to Bogotá,

Colombia, as the lowest-level political officer in the embassy. No rhyme, no reason. The big machine just churned out names and slots.

More years and assignments passed, and I was very unhappy about my career. I seriously began to ponder leaving the Foreign Service and trying something new. Thanks to a wonderful Foreign Service contact from my days in Bogotá, I was assigned a State Department Congressional Fellowship, which meant spending a year on Capitol Hill.

At the end of that year, when Senator Max Baucus offered me the job of legislative director, I resigned without hesitation from the Foreign Service. Perhaps the Foreign Service could offer me opportunities to study political events (at risk of not getting promoted), but here in Washington DC I was immersed in the process itself. Suddenly things really mattered. You weren't merely satisfying some nameless bureaucrat far away but dealing with issues of importance in determining the course of the nation.

My quitting one career and starting something entirely new surely chagrined my father, who had lived and been raised on the principles of having one steady job throughout one's life, working hard, getting promoted, and achieving success through loyalty and dedication to the system. It had worked so well for him. He had spent twenty-five years as Swiss consul and consul general in New York (one of Switzerland's most important posts, since the very survival and livelihood of the Swiss depended on world trade). That was followed by fifteen years as ambassador to Canada. His was a pretty good career path to emulate—and I had tried.

After five years in Congress, I started to look forward more and more to something I had never before considered too seriously: getting out of the great bureaucracy and being my own boss. Boy, did that sound exciting and challenging—almost unbelievable. But that's what happened. In 1982, I left my job in Congress for the great unknown.

It was one of the bravest decisions of my life.

I started looking for a business I could go into. I investigated lots of opportunities. Book publishing particularly appealed to me, since I had always enjoyed reading, and I thought working on the production of a book would be challenging and stimulating. It fell a bit far outside my realm, and ultimately I chickened out. All I knew was that I wanted my own business and did not want to work for someone else.

The break came in 1986. I was perusing the "Businesses for Sale" section of the newspaper classifieds when I noticed a small ad: Language School for Sale. I spoke foreign languages. I had studied foreign languages. I felt comfortable with the subject matter and at home with foreigners.

Languages had always come easily to me. My father spoke French to me from birth, and my mother spoke Polish. My sister and I spoke English to each other, with friends, and at school. Over time, my proficiency in foreign languages inevitably declined for lack of constant practice, but my abilities remained decent, generally at a colloquial level. The intricacies of grammar were easier to learn, because I maintained a speaking proficiency.

Knowledge of foreign languages had been a big help in the Foreign Service, and I had had no qualms whatsoever when sent off to learn Spanish, where my proficiency eventually equaled my ease with French. I honestly never gave it much thought. So I spoke French—so what? It was my natural state of being.

It is important to remember the basis of language learning: Speak it, listen to it, absorb it without even thinking about it. This is particularly true when you learn a language as a child. I was naturally tri-lingual at age four.

I called the seller of the language school, who turned out to be a Frenchman living in Philadelphia. He had started the school but had tired of it and seemed inclined to return to France or do something else. We met, we negotiated, and there I was, the owner of a small, four-classroom language school.

It felt a bit scary, but I'm not sure I realized how scary it really was. I knew nothing about running a business, book-keeping, hiring personnel, finding new contracts, and so on. Yet there I was, totally on my own, sink or swim.

The language school I bought was part of an international school-licensing organization called *inlingua*. The schools were all owner-owned. It was not a franchise, but the owner received a license which gave you rights to use *inlingua* books and testing materials and participate in organizational activities, like school congresses and book development. They insisted that you use only their books and materials.

Fortunately for me, the sale included a commitment on my part to assure employment of the staff who were there, so right from the start I had a cadre of people who knew what they were doing. The most helpful was the director of the school.

Since it was always my intention to run the school myself (otherwise, what would I do?), I let the director go after four months. That time had been well spent, since I learned the mechanics of operating a business and the special substantive aspects of this particular business. The man who lost his job didn't seem to mind too much, and he promptly went off on a year's sabbatical.

A new owner had to understand how the *inlingua* system worked: four months of six-hour days. Sure enough, at the end of the course (assuming some natural ear for foreign sounds), a student could engage in simple conversations and understand what was being said at whatever level he had signed up for. That is what the school sold the prospective student. Success or failure was easy to discern. The system worked, and students, for the most part, did achieve their language speaking goals.

Now I had to begin hiring staff. Language schools such as mine have a naturally large turnover in staff, as most teachers are independent contractors. One might teach a language to a student for two, four, or six months. If the student passed the required test (usually a US Government test), the class was over. Good-bye, teacher, at least until another class popped up.

The school might seek a different teacher of the same language because a certain accent was sought or a dialect might be needed. We were constantly on the lookout for teachers. Many were returnees, maybe having worked at another school for a while but out on the market again. It was fairly easy to find the right teacher, since there was a large pool of them in the DC area.

Unusual languages could cause difficulties or time delays, but there was not much that could be done about it. An impatient student was free to go to another school, but that school would be facing the same problem. Our well-trained and experienced staff supervisors were themselves often former teachers who really knew the business and would almost always find a solution. If they couldn't, it was doubtful another school would do better.

A language school is not like any other business. One inevitably became closely involved with people—teachers and students—and one had to enjoy doing that. It involved understanding the difficulties for the students and the different cultural backgrounds of the teachers. A sympathetic ear was most valuable.

I was fortunate when one day Deidre Doyle came knocking at my door looking for work. She was a business broker and experienced in small-business operation. She, too, wanted to be actively involved in running a company. She knew what was needed to manage a successful business, and that was what I needed badly. I hired her as my deputy.

Deidre stayed in that position for the next fifteen years and helped grow the company to become, by far, the largest private language-school in the metropolitan area. We developed contracts with or served just about every government agency, from small organizations, such as the Patent Office, to the very largest, such as the Department of Defense and its Defense Language Institute. We worked with the Drug Enforcement Agency, the State Department's Foreign Service Institute, the Commerce Department, the Foreign Agricultural Service, the National Security Agency, and others.

I tried to make the school fun and interesting. We threw birthday parties, big Christmas parties, and took our senior staff on a yearly trip for a few days of working seminars. We went to Las Vegas, Florida, and Bermuda. People liked working for us.

I think we were so successful for a variety of reasons.

First, government reps recognized me as "one of theirs," as a long-time career Foreign Service officer and thus trustworthy from the point of view of government security and that sort of thing. Most of the competition was owned by ex-teachers, foreigners, or individuals not connected to or knowledgeable about government.

Yet almost by definition, operating such a school in Washington, DC meant working closely with the government. The government bureaucrats were more comfortable dealing with us, knowing that our "pedigree" was good.

Second, I suspect my considerable connection to the US Senate helped. I had learned that government people had an inherent discomfort and even fear of any involvement with Congress. But here I was, with that experience, basically on their side.

Third, it surely helped a great deal with the Department of Defense that my deputy, Deidre, came from a military family. Her husband was an active lieutenant colonel in the Army. Once we started operating, we found that such camaraderie and fellowship could be important in establishing friendly relations with military contracting officers. In a way, she spoke their language. The Defense Language Institute ended up being our biggest client.

And fourth, perhaps of lesser importance but still a factor, was my own extensive experience with foreign languages and living abroad. I knew what the students had to cope with in their onward assignments. I was a sympathetic ear, helping students achieve their goals for service in a foreign land.

Deidre lacked foreign language experience or serious time spent abroad outside an Army base. But she did know something about contracting, book keeping, and the administrative aspects of running a business, which helped tremendously.

We made a pretty effective combination, and the school grew rapidly. Always trying to be helpful to our clients, we expanded locally. We opened a branch near Ft. Meade to better service the NSA. We sent teachers to more isolated posts so that students would not have to travel far to attend class. I even moved our head offices from the District to Rosslyn, Virginia, to be closer to the Pentagon and the State Department (its Foreign Service Institute had a headquarters in Virginia).

It always surprised me the extent to which my old home agency, the State Department, ended up using our services. After all, the Foreign Service Institute was the venerated granddaddy of language schools, preparing foreign service people for their tours abroad. I had attended FSI courses on several occasions, such as a valuable brush-up course in Spanish, prior to assignment in Guatemala.

The reason they used my school was, I believe, typically bureaucratic. As the world changed, and the US extended its reach to many new areas where relatively unknown foreign languages were spoken, the government often found itself unable to react quickly to the demand. For example, the department suddenly needed teachers of unusual languages like Amharic or Tagalog, not to speak of Arabic and its many dialects. The government hiring process was often bogged down by requirements for security clearances, etc., which are time-consuming. But the individual needed the training right away.

The answer for the State Department was, of course, to use independent contractors. We could search for, hire, and train teachers for those languages so much more quickly. We had some teachers who were full-time employees highly experienced in dealing with special issues, but they would at times leave us for another school that could use their expertise on a temporary contract. We did the same, and everyone was happy. Very rarely did we have to do any special training, and only when it involved a little-known language.

This must have embarrassed the State Department, so I suspect they devised a strategy to avoid looking like they couldn't provide instruction themselves. They let us hire teachers and run the class. But the class would physically take place in the State Department building so they could say it was a State Department class. They reimbursed us all our expenses. It made little difference to me. We did the work, trained and tested all the students, and were paid accordingly. In fact, it saved us real estate expenses.

I confess that sometimes the teacher search was challenging. Imagine being asked to find a qualified teacher to teach someone going overseas a language so remote almost no one has ever heard of it. The search could go far afield, but somehow we would find at least one person somewhere who knew it—either a relative of someone working at the embassy, or an itinerant student.

We then had to give the new hires crash courses in teaching the *inlingua* method and find books in the language. Believe it or not, some languages did not have any written books at all, so we had

inlingua *headquarters staff*

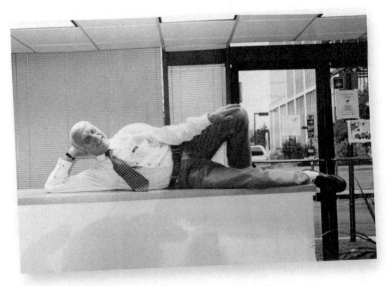

*Relaxing at the entrance of my
renovated school in Washington.*

to write rudimentary text books. We would assign an experienced *inlingua* teacher (in another language) to work closely with the class to assure the teaching methods were best applied. Everyone worked hard, and usually the student understood the tremendous challenge. There was little choice. No one else, including the government, could do any better.

We steadily grew and soon had three branch schools in the area. Here I also learned for the first time how some businesses worked in a cut-throat world. One disgruntled competitor tried to set us up to be kicked out of government contracting. Our contract said that if we opened and moved to a new campus without informing the government, we would be in breach of the contract. So this man accused us of illegally opening a new campus.

Upon investigation, the government was surprised to learn that the "new campus" was a small suite of additional offices we had briefly rented within our building to take care of additional students the government had sent us. The disgruntled competitor hoped the government would buy his accusations that this was a campus, and we'd be cooked. Neither he nor the government expected we would hire a lawyer and dare to fight.

Such were the fabricated accusations (twenty-four of them!) thrown at us, and we needed to disprove them entirely. It was very disturbing that the government would even listen to such complaints from individuals who were obviously struggling competitors set on destroying us. I learned that the business world ain't so sweet and the government often a highly indifferent moderator. We emerged victorious, only somewhat poorer, having been forced to use lawyers to make our case.

The company I licensed with, *inlingua*, was Eurocentric and paid little attention to all the other languages of the world. For all the European schools in the *inlingua* network—about eighty percent of the schools—that was not a big problem, since they taught mostly European languages. But we Americans had to look further afield, particularly for Asian and Latin American languages. There were no *inlingua* books or other materials available for many of those. *inlingua* criticized us and tried to forbid us to use outside material (the license agreement obliged us to use only *inlingua* books). But they couldn't really stop us. We had to find books outside the *inlingua* library if we wanted to serve all of our customers.

We became leaders in an ad hoc revolutionary group within the *inlingua* system that ignored the *inlingua* rules and used whatever worked to teach whatever language was called for. That didn't earn me any favors with those who ran the place. *inlingua* was founded by a German and the German influence was the greatest. They did little more than harass us from time to time. They were loath to throw out a segment of their licensees who were making good profits, paying full license fees, and growing the *inlingua* name and reputation worldwide.

But they didn't mind setting roadblocks or causing nuisances. I wanted to open a school in Japan and went to considerable effort to do that. When I applied for a license for Japan, the big bosses said no. They said they did not want to expand to Japan, even though it was the biggest growth market in the world. It was, I'm sure, an anti-American (me) motivation. One could see naked nationalism at work, even if it cost them. They did eventually give in, but they made it difficult for a while.

In the years since I had joined the *inlingua* network, we had become the largest licensee with the most schools in the whole *inlingua* system. We got there by challenging their silly restrictions, their Eurocentric state of mind, and their great conservatism. We had several hundred teachers, well over 100 classrooms, and were teaching more than 110 languages to thousands of students each year. It galled them, I believe, that an American school was number one. But we made good money for them and for us.

At one of the annual *inlingua* congresses, a discussion began about the whole system. I spoke rather passionately about the need to adjust and open up. When I finished, to my great surprise, the place erupted in thunderous applause. There were about 150 *inlingua* schools world-wide at that time, and the other owners were clearly on my side. It must have pained the old school!

Not too long after that, a rather informal and unannounced request came to me from headquarters. Could I help find appropriate textbooks to teach those languages for which *inlingua* did not have materials? They also rather sheepishly agreed to let me produce a Japanese textbook that became the official text for *inlingua*. I was fortunate to have on my staff a very bright Japanese scholar who took on the task with relish and did a great job. The old school finally accepted that it had to change. I believe it is still using our text.

My Foreign Service background made it hard for me to ignore the international possibilities of *inlingua*'s network, since I always was a person who feels comfortable in an international milieu. So eventually and inevitably, I began to think about opening a school abroad, somewhere *inlingua* did not have a presence.

By chance, one of my Japanese teachers was the very nice wife of the deputy chief of mission at the US embassy in Tokyo. Peggy Breer was a true Japanophile. She knew Japan better than most experts and spoke fluent Japanese. When she heard of my expansionist interests, she suggested I come to Japan and she would help me. She and her husband were due to return to their assignment in Tokyo. Although married to the DCM, nothing would forbid her from volunteering her skills to help a private American school.

It worked beautifully. She used her extensive contacts in Japan and knowledge of that nation to land a contract for me with the Mitsui Corporation, which was looking to open an in-house English language training center. Soon we were in business. I hired a young American woman who had been studying in Japan to serve as my manager.

I never regretted the decision, although I was frequently frustrated by having to work within a Japanese structure under the strict Japanese rules of office behavior. When the boss walked in, everyone jumped to his feet. Still, it was fun to observe and learn. The Japanese proved to be delightful people to work with, despite a rigid caste structure and general lack of personal initiative. Of course, all this went against the earlier *inlingua* decision not to allow me to have a school in Japan. By now they had admitted defeat and raised no objections.

My new career gave me very rewarding experiences for twenty-five years. I'm sure I would not have been as successful had I not thoroughly enjoyed the challenge of education. It was so satisfying to see people grow under my tutelage, and to realize how my actions could positively affect the lives of so many people.

There was also much personal satisfaction seeing the success I had achieved: from just four or five classrooms to entire schools in East Asia, Southeast Asia, and the US, providing language training to thousands of students in well over a hundred languages. At the end I was able to sell the schools for substantially more than they had cost me. Not bad. It was an exciting time. I was my own boss, out from under layers of government bureaucrats.

I decided that I had made one of the wisest decisions of my life.

Opening my school with my
Japanese colleagues in Tokyo.

chapter two

From Mongolia
to Vietnam

My effort to open a school in Japan had provided me an invaluable experience. It was the beginning of what became the most enjoyable part of my life—the lure of opening English language schools abroad. At the time, Japan seemed like a bit of a fluke, brought to me by someone from the outside, not my doing. I only vaguely thought of other ventures abroad.

Then, serendipity: One day someone from the State Department called me to set up an appointment with some visiting Mongolian government officials. The Mongolian Ministry of Energy was interested in sending some of their staff to the US for English-language training. English had gradually become the world's lingua franca. Everyone wanted—needed—to learn it. Would I be interested?

It seemed really fortuitous for two reasons. I was excited by the thought of training foreign government officials, but from Mongolia? Wow. I had never served in Asia as a Foreign Service officer, and never even visited any Asian country other than Japan. But I had always had this picture of Mongolia: distant, isolated, challenged, a land of nomads and big adventures, Genghis Khan. And I was actually going to meet people from there!

I wasn't a shoo-in. The Mongolian officials had come to interview a number of schools for English as a Second Language classes for twelve to fifteen officials. My school taught all languages, including ESL, but ESL was not a large part of the curriculum. I suspect Al LaPorta, a wonderful man and our outstanding ambassador in Ulaan Bataar, may have helped them make up their minds.

I had no idea whether I had any chance at all, but the gods were good to me, and the officials selected my school. Next thing I knew, some fifteen Mongolian officials anxious to learn English were on my doorstep.

I felt honored and pleased. They were a bright and enthusiastic group. I may have made them feel more comfortable during our initial meeting by expressing my strong desire to visit their land and learn what I could about it. I also told them of my experiences opening a school in various other locations, including Japan, so I knew what their needs would be.

Most intriguing to me was a new thought that came to my mind. If they really wanted to start a big program to train their employees to learn English, what if I offered to go to Mongolia and open a school there? Think how much money that would save them. At that point I was naïve enough not even to think of the possibility that the Mongolians were more interested in traveling to the US on government money than in learning English. That's not entirely fair, as most of them did apply themselves to their studies. But still, a trip and stay in the US was undoubtedly very appealing.

It took a while to make them think realistically of my offer. Luckily, Ambassador LaPorta liked the idea of an American school in Mongolia. When we went over to Mongolia to explore possibilities, he immediately greeted me warmly. In the months to come, he helped us enormously by opening doors and proposing procedures to follow. My having been a Foreign Service officer surely helped. We would be the first English language school and an important educational presence in a country just emerging from Soviet-Communist domination.

I have to admit to a bit of brash self-confidence. I was so taken by the extreme attractiveness of the land and its people that I looked forward with endless enthusiasm to the challenges and excitement of this new adventure, so foreign and different. It never occurred to me that it might not work! Also, I believe that my mixture of foreign and domestic upbringing made me a bit immune to suspicion of foreign ventures. They didn't feel so foreign to me.

Thanks to Ambassador LaPorta, I found myself meeting lots of Mongolians who were most interested in this new investor. Before long, I was looking for someone to manage a school I might start, and a suitable location for it.

I also made the important decision that this was going to be *my* school, not an *inlingua* license. I now knew enough about running a school that I did not need the assistance of European overlords. This one would be called Santis Educational Services (SES), named for Säntis, the highest mountain in eastern Switzerland near which many of my early ancestors were raised. Nothing to do with schools, languages or anything else; I just thought it would be a quaint name.

I hired a bright young graduate of one of the Peace Corps' first programs in Mongolia and rented space in a centrally located office building in Ulaan Baatar. Soon we were off and running. I had fun finding English teachers, more former Peace Corps volunteers but also itinerant US college grads and spouses of US officials. I found lots of perfectly good (maybe better than *inlingua*'s) books we could use to train our new students.

We also found a nice little side-line teaching foreigners the Mongolian language. We taught individuals at the US diplomatic mission; local employees learned English, and American employees learned Mongolian.

It is very embarrassing to admit that even though I traveled to Mongolia constantly, I never mastered the language. All my staff spoke good English and were always around to interpret for me. I tried to learn, and I would pick up phrases and practice them. Alas, I would come home and weeks would go by without any opportunity to use those phrases. I was always going back to square one. Also, Mongolian is a very different language to learn for a native English speaker: different sounds, no common roots, different grammars, and so on. It's not like going from one Romance language to another.

Other government contracts started to come in. One of the first was teaching English to employees of the Mongolian Aviation Authority. More and more planes were flying over this remote nation, and more and more planes were flying in businessmen and other investors as Mongolia's economy was discovered.

The country had only in recent times emerged from the grips of communism, but long before that, there was Genghis Khan. In 1206, he successfully pulled together various independent tribes in northern Mongolia to form the nucleus of what became the state of Mongolia. He organized his people into an effective fighting force which proceeded to conquer most of northern Asia. He never succeeded in conquering the Japanese, but he did extend his rule from the Pacific to central Europe. The empire he created was one of the largest in all history. To do so, he established a remarkable administrative structure to rule his dynasty.

He was feared as a ruthless opponent; he was known to execute every inhabitant of a town or city that fought or opposed him. He also gave his subjects many benefits, supported freedom of religion, and encouraged international trade. Today he is praised as a fairly enlightened leader who developed warfare techniques, such as his use of cavalry, which pulverized those he fought. He was rightfully feared by his enemies but admired by his people.

After his death, Genghis Khan's influence lasted for several generations. Mongolia eventually fell under the sway of the Soviet Union until the 1990s, when some degree of democracy arrived. Mongolia struggled to adapt to the modern economic system. To move into the 20th century, the country began to exploit its enormous natural resources.

Mongolia's nomadic population still exists in greatly reduced numbers; it has decreased from eighty percent to maybe thirty percent. Mongolians have adapted to the modern world with its growth, corruption, environmental and urban pollution, and democratic procedures. Unlike many of its neighbors, Mongolia's remarkably free and fair elections have carried the nation forward.

Our very first staff at our school in Mongolia.

Mongolia is one of the richest countries in Asia as far as natural resources are concerned. Eventually, it had the largest copper mine and biggest coal reserves in Asia, not to speak of rare earth minerals, gold, silver, and so on. Mongolia's earlier Communist masters refused to exploit the country's natural resources lest it make Mongolians too self-assertive.

Up until this time, when working overseas, I remained within the cocoon of American culture. Work friends were American; the office atmosphere was American. My work contacts, while usually foreign, were still representatives of their own societies.

In Mongolia it was different, as I established myself in a totally foreign environment. I had no parent embassy and staff to huddle with. Daily life was regulated by how the local people behaved, not how we behaved. Their reactions to events were determined by their culture, not mine.

After about a year building the business in Mongolia, I wondered why no one had told me anything about how to pay taxes. I went down to the revenue office and asked, "How do I pay taxes?" The fellow gave me a strange look, then asked, "But aren't you a school?" He told me schools did not pay taxes in Mongolia. When I told him I was a privately-owned company, not a government entity, he said that was not possible.

Well, I didn't want to argue too hard. We left it that he would check further and let me know. Of course, I soon heard from him. There followed a discussion where I explained our system was not like the Soviet one which had existed for the last seventy years in Mongolia.

He was very happy to hear my explanations, and it didn't take long for them to produce a tax code that could apply to me. I was sorry in a way that I hadn't kept my mouth shut, but I honestly felt it the right thing to do. Mongolia was going to learn about western capitalism sooner or later, and it was better that I be on the side of the angels.

To accomplish my objectives, I had to travel constantly to Mongolia, often staying for several weeks at a time. It would have been much easier simply to move there for an extended period, but I did have my businesses in the US to watch over, as they too grew. I also had a family to support, and I really did not want to leave them for such long periods of time.

Mongolians are very bright, hard-working, loyal, and anxious to succeed. I never felt uncomfortable leaving them in charge while I travelled. Upon my return, I would always be amazed by their dedication to the school and our objectives. Making things still easier, I was fortunate to be able to attract Mongolians relatively fluent in English. So I never had any language problems.

We grew and grew, and soon we needed bigger space. I decided we would build our own school, and what an adventure that was. I learned so much about the corruption inherent in any operation and found myself facing down ministers who tried to sway us for just about anything. It was not uncommon to have a minister or other high official expect us to give them passing grades on their

The new inlingua *building in Ulaan Baatar, Mongolia, which we built in 1999. It was the first private language school in Mongolia.*

language tests no matter how badly they performed. We lost a lot of business, but thankfully we also gained a good reputation that served us well.

In another instance, we bid for a large contract to train United Nations employees. It was a pretty standard contract, similar to ones we fielded back home, and we were pretty confident in our response. No Mongolian competitor had anywhere near the know-how to bid appropriately. When the award came out, it went to the wife of the minister of education, who didn't even own a school. This was the minister who had been charged with making the award on behalf of the UN.

I was furious. It offended my fundamental sense of ethics. But I had been around long enough to know it was useless to challenge their actions at a time like this. I immediately appealed the award to UN headquarters in New York, and they began an investigation. To make a long story short, the minister suddenly withdrew the whole contract and declared it might be re-offered sometime in the future. This was after the minister called me into his office to suggest that if I dropped my appeal, other business would come my way.

What probably saved me was that I was a foreigner, an American, and owner of the largest private school in Mongolia. I think they were a bit intimidated. Nothing ever happened to me, and life went on. Even the Ministry of Education eventually came back to us. I think probably they were frightened by the UN, which must have demanded to know what was going on.

More ominous and potentially more dangerous things also occurred. At one point, when I was going through the process of constructing our school building, I ran headlong into a rather nasty fight with the neighbor to my site. He happened to be one of Mongolia's biggest sports stars, the national wrestling champion. I had been awarded by the mayor's office a plot of land on which to build, but this fellow suddenly appeared and claimed the land was his.

He was a burly fellow, what one would expect a wrestler to look like. Typical of many Mongolians, he could be absolutely charming and non-threatening, but in the bat of an eye, he could look like someone you hoped you'd never meet alone on a dark street. He actually had his own sports training facility literally across the street from our school. As a sports star, he was greatly admired by the general population, making it even more difficult to challenge him. We were in a suburban business neighborhood—a University branch across another street, a school down the road—peaceful enough and not threatening.

I actually went to court over this one, and naturally lost. How could I win against a national sports hero? But here the mayor's office and other officials came to my rescue, and I was awarded the land, albeit reduced in size to accommodate the sports star.

The day came when construction crews arrived to start work. To our surprise and consternation, the wrestler had a whole bunch of hired toughs standing around, ready to stop construction by intimidation. Cops were all around, but not one even lifted a finger to protect our crews. The wrestlers' friends blocked everything. They even set up barriers. Needless to say, the construction crews hightailed it out of there.

I went out into the middle of our plot and did not let anyone go further, all the while the cops just stood around. Then the wrestler's foreman or someone like that arrived in his car. He drove very slowly, but straight at me. I did not move. His fender finally touched my leg, and with a big shout, I fell dramatically on the hood of his car, seriously denting it (very cheap car, heavy human).

I was not hurt, since the fall was for drama, not the result of the contact with his fender. I was relieved when a good American friend who was accompanying us grabbed a big brick and discreetly stuck it under the wheel of the car so it could not move. This all played out like a silent movie—no words exchanged, just people doing things.

The crowd mysteriously melted away, and just a few of us were left standing in the middle of our grounds. Peace and quiet reigned. Everyone retreated to their corners to meet again more sedately in the future. The upshot was that we did get to build our school, the wrestler agreed to the land distribution, and soon we were installed in our spanking new quarters. He ended up being not a bad neighbor.

The episode was scary, but I understood the Mongolian character well enough not to worry too much. Mongolians can be very gentle and thoughtful people. Just a little while earlier, I had challenged them by starting to tear down a fence they had built between our two properties. A huge Mongolian immediately approached me, but in so gentle a manner. No, he didn't want me to do that, and he took the fence out of my hands and gently laid it aside. I honestly think that I was always safe. There is great Mongolian reverence for the elderly, and I qualified for that, even if I did try to tear down a fence.

By this time my ex-Peace Corps volunteer director had long departed. His successor, another former volunteer, had also departed. Both were good men, but perhaps a bit young and the challenge too large. Then we had as deputy director, Orgilmaa Doloonjin, a rock-solid Mongolian woman who spoke fluent English and had studied in the US and Japan. She had been hired by the first director and, given the shortcomings of the two young men, ended up being the anchor for the school. She essentially ran it for them.

Her background and subsequent accomplishments also fascinated me. She had been born to a nomad family and spent the first eighteen years of her life growing up in the middle of the Gobi Desert, living in *gers* (tents). She not only survived but actually successfully educated herself and grew into a strong and ambitious woman. So it was without too much hesitation that I appointed her the new director, a position she held until the very end of my tenure, at which time she purchased the school from me. I was so happy in the ensuing years to see the school prosper and grow under her management—a true success story.

I went to Mongolia with the express intent to help the nation grow, which I think I did in a very small and individual way. It was always my secret desire to create something that would flourish and could be passed on to a truly deserving person. When I sold the operation to my successor, the terms of sale were well below market price and designed mostly to make sure the new owner would not be starting with large debts. Normal financial matters had to be dealt with generously or else nothing would ever happen.

The school I started in Ulaan Baatar was the first privately-owned school in the country. At first, the very concept of a privately-owned school was hard for the people to imagine, but it ended up being the largest and best school around. I am very proud of that and of its successful change of hands. The transfer was seamless and without publicity.

While I served in the Foreign Service, the world was consumed by the horrors of the Vietnam War. I felt so sorry for all involved: the many innocent Vietnamese who suffered or were killed, the many Americans killed or wounded fighting a war that many opposed. It was a relief when hostilities finally ended.

I never imagined that Vietnam would become an important part of my career. Simply by chance, as a result of an international educational conference, I became acquainted with a Vietnamese woman who indicated an interest in opening a language school in her hometown of Hanoi. Once again, I got interested in opening another school. She worked as an agent who sought students in Vietnam who wanted to study abroad. Since she had no experience in running a school, she was looking for an experienced partner.

After exchanging some correspondence, I decided to visit Vietnam to meet the people and see how realistic the possibilities were. Frankly, I was worried. After all, we had been at war not too long before. What chance did I have for a friendly and fair reception, the owner of an American school who wanted to start a school in Hanoi teaching English?

The woman, Thuy Thu Do, turned out to be most gracious and generous. She really wanted to start a school and thought that my participation would be a big plus for her. So we went ahead, formed a collaboration, and soon we had a functioning school in Hanoi. Miracle of miracles, her predictions were right on. Never once did anyone make reference to the war; in fact, one memorable response was, "That was then. Now you are here."

As it turned out, the school was a constant source of strange occurrences. For example, a government official might suddenly decree that we needed to pay a heavy fine for not observing a zoning rule. Everything would grind to a stop. Thuy would smile and be gone, returning a little later to tell me it was all settled. "A mistake," giggle, giggle.

I soon learned that when we visited an official, Thuy would often unobtrusively leave behind a little unmarked envelope. It usually contained a small amount of cash. This practice kept us out of trouble, and officials were glad to see us. Large amounts were not involved; "tip money," we might call it.

I never knew what my partner was going to do next, and it could be a struggle to keep up with her if I didn't keep my sense of humor. Thuy seemed to think I was sort of weird for expecting some predictability to our operation. I never knew what was coming next.

Thuy seemed well connected, and whenever something would happen that I was sure would end us all in trouble, she would just laugh and somehow take care of it. I suspected she solved problems the Vietnamese way, with envelopes stuffed with cash, but her connections surely played a big role, too.

She also liked to travel and was always glad to go somewhere "for an inspection." Thuy liked to take me along to show me off as her American business partner. Of course, being highly family-oriented, she always brought along family members: her sisters, husband, daughter, and Lord knows who. I got to know her family and learned a lot about Vietnamese family customs and traditions. It was fun to be treated as almost a family member. To this day, some of her family remain close friends. Just recently, my wife and I were invited to the sumptuous wedding of Thuy's niece, Nicki, in the Washington area.

Thuy and her family often acted as guides as I traveled all over Vietnam. We went from the Chinese border way up north all the way down to the Mekong Delta, from the western borders with Laos and Cambodia to beautiful eastern beaches along the South China Sea. Fortunately, my family likes to travel, and most times my family, or at least parts of it, would also come along. They were often very helpful. My daughters are all involved in education, and their insights and experiences contributed greatly.

A couple of trips impacted me powerfully. The most moving and heart-wrenching was a visit to Laos, where I visited the killing fields and horrible prisons set up by Pol Pot and the Khmer Rouge. They had killed several million people in most brutal ways, and destroyed a whole generation of their population—a truly tragic and awesome place to visit.

The city of Luang Prabang is impossible to forget. Babies and small children in detention centers were executed by simply swinging them by their feet, headfirst against a huge tree, which still stands in the killing fields. The place is filled with human skulls and shallow burial grounds. Torture chambers still stand. Shocking in my view, to this day *not one* person has been held responsible for these atrocities. How humans can be so barbaric to their fellow man, I'll never understand.

Then we visited Cambodia, with its fantastic historic palaces at Phnom Penh. We visited incredible ancient carvings covering hundreds of acres, some overgrown with jungle. I will always remember these as some of the most moving and historically fascinating places I have ever visited. Part of what made it all so intriguing for me was the fact that it was part of Asian culture, about which I knew so little. It was all "new" history to me.

Founding schools abroad opened up a whole new world to me, a world filled with fine people and lovely locations and different food, customs, and habits. Students at the schools were usually highly-motivated employees of the local government. It was thoroughly enjoyable and challenging to teach English to such motivated individuals, most of whom had never studied a language other than their own.

Now they suddenly had to learn English, as pending assignments would take them to places where English was the lingua franca. It was a challenge for very serious students in a country where learning a foreign language was not part of a normal curriculum. To this day, I miss that life very much.

By the time I left that business after twenty-five years, we were the largest private language school in the DC area, with three locations in the Greater DC area and branch schools in Tokyo, Ulaan Baatar, and Hanoi.

Buying the language school had marked the beginning of the happiest time in my life. I had lived in a self-created structure. In other words, I was my own boss, undertaking projects created by my own thinking, and responsible for my own successes and failures. No longer was I tied to government (or anyone else's) schedules or managed by supervisors.

How did I wind up with such an entrepreneurial spirit? Maybe it has something to do with the intrigue and excitement in the lives of my ancestors in Europe. From enormous wealth to genteel poverty, foot-loose adventure, nobility, murder, espionage, and mixing it up with Napoleon, I come from some lively stock. The next chapter explores my family history.

chapter three

Family History

My sister and I were born in the US as American citizens of foreign parents. My dad was a Swiss Protestant, my mom a Polish Catholic. My sister and I both had dual citizenship with Switzerland.

For twenty-five years, my parents resided in New York City, and grew to love it. My sister and I always considered ourselves New Yorkers, as did my parents, especially my mother. My father, because of his official position, had to be a bit aloof. But in private, my mother especially loved to claim she was a New Yorker.

Both my father's and mother's ancestries were relatively unknown to me growing up. Our ancestry was never much discussed, unless we went to Switzerland for a family reunion or some such event. Then we would see family trees and hear a bit about who was what and who did what. As I grew older (and I mean really older), I began to realize that actually my ancestors were some pretty unusual folk.

Unfortunately, World War II had caused an almost total rupture in our communications with my mother's relatives in Poland. We heard how one of my aunts had been a member of the Polish Underground against the Nazis, and how my cousin as a young boy had fled from his home and hidden in the woods when the Nazis came knocking at the door. He apparently fled more permanently to the countryside where he remained throughout the war in relative hiding and obscurity. We heard little else. Even my mother's original birth records were destroyed by fire.

Just by chance, I came across an article in the *New York Times* on July 28, 2018, that gave meaning to the suffering the Polish people endured. It commemorates the Warsaw Uprising seventy-four years earlier, which it describes as "one of the most heroic acts of bravery that ever took place."

"This was one of the largest and cruelest mass executions . . . during WWII. The occupying Germans mercilessly murdered civilians. The Soviet Army (supposedly allied with the Western anti-Nazi forces) was positioned east of Central Warsaw and remained idle [and] refused to let Western Allies use Soviet air bases to airlift supplies. Russians only entered Warsaw three months after the uprising was squelched." It is no wonder my mother had such strong feelings about the war.

After the war, my mother, taking my sister with her, traveled there. It was risky and very hard; the Communists were in firm control, and my mother would never have been able to go were it not for her Swiss diplomatic passport. She came back with a few stories, but she did not seem eager to talk too much about it. It must have been a terrible shock for her to witness her homeland so destroyed and taken over by the Soviets.

She did mention that one of her uncles, who had been an officer in the Polish army, was arrested by the Soviets and sent off to a Russian gulag. He was not seen nor heard from for twenty years. He apparently reappeared, having been finally released by the Soviets and deemed old and harmless. No one recognized him at first when he knocked and entered the family home.

To her dying day, my mother had an intense dislike for the Germans and Russians. When the Army sent me to Germany, she lived in mortal fear that I would return with a young Fräulein on my arm. She would have never forgiven me had I bought a German car. This animosity was bred by the enormous fear she had for the safety of her family during the war. There was literally no news available in New York about the events in Eastern Europe. For five years, she had to live not knowing what was happening, but with plenty of information regarding Nazi atrocities. When she finally did get to return briefly to Poland after the war, she heard so many stories of the miseries her family suffered that it was very hard for her to be forgiving.

The family heritage home had been a large mansion in Warsaw. My mother's family was a noble one; my grandfather was Count Mostowski. The family consisted of nine children, my mother one of the younger ones. One day (well before the war), one of the relatives was being married in a big ceremony at the ancestral home. Suddenly a shot rang out, and one of the guests staggered out from one of the rooms. "Help!" he must have cried, "the Count is dead!" The story passed down through the years was that the man was showing my grandfather a new pistol, and it accidentally discharged while they were examining it, striking my grandfather and killing him.

After relations warmed and the Berlin Wall came down, it was finally possible to reunite with our Polish relatives. My cousin Remi, son of my mother's sister, not only came to Switzerland, but we also invited him and members of his family to the US. His mother had been my mom's closest sibling.

Remi did not speak English, a language the Communists did not encourage, but he did know some French. Between my broken Polish and our mutual knowledge of French, we were able to communicate satisfactorily. It was very emotional and touching to reestablish contact after so many years. I was only sorry that my mother had passed away a few years earlier.

My cousin Remi told me the story of how, as a young boy, he had been forced to witness the torture death of a young Pole by the Germans. Apparently the young Pole was shot by a security guard or someone like that as he walked across the village square. He crumpled to the ground, tried to get up, but could not. Other Poles rushed to help him but were greeted by gunfire. So the young man just lay there, in the middle of the village square, in plain sight of everybody, until he died. The Germans walked away, leaving his body to be disposed of by others—a horrifying scene for a young boy to have witnessed.

My mother's maiden name was Mostowska, but since her family was noble, the French add a "de" to the name to designate rank. So, in French-speaking parts of Europe, or in other countries with links to nobility, my mom became Maria de Mostowska. My parents rarely used the "de" in her name. In fact, it wasn't until long into my adulthood that I even knew that form of her name. It was always simply Mr. and Mrs. Victor Nef, or Maria Nef.

My mother was a real proletarian and did not like all that stuff. She liked to think she was a woman of the people, and never once did I hear her talk about that aspect of her family. As far as I know, never in her life did she use the "de" on her own. We used to tease her and joke that she was just another left-winger.

With the passing of various relatives, communication with the extended family, which was difficult anyway, almost petered out entirely. We learned that the ancestral home had been seized by the Communists and turned into some sort of official home. It still stands in Warsaw, but no one has been back recently or been able to find or photograph it.

Personally, I have a few childhood memories which have clung with me, and which have helped me think of my Polish background. One of those memories is of the visit to our apartment of Jan Karski (his nom de guerre) in about 1945. At that time, he was one of the brave leaders of the Polish resistance against the Germans and one of the Christians who helped lead the struggle against the Holocaust.

Karski was taken prisoner by the Germans in 1939, but on his way to a POW camp, he managed to escape to join one of the first resistance movements. There he formed the first courier missions from inside Poland to supporters in the West. On one of these courier missions, he was arrested by the Gestapo and severely tortured. With the help of fellow resistance fighters, he again escaped, was smuggled out, and eventually returned to Polish army headquarters.

In 1942, Karski was tasked with reporting to Polish leaders and Allies about Nazi atrocities in occupied Poland. To gather evidence, he was once again smuggled into the Warsaw Ghetto by Jewish leaders to observe what was happening to Polish Jews. His reporting provided the Allies with the first evidence of the horrors inflicted on Polish Jews.

Once back in the West in 1943, he reported widely on his findings, briefing many party and other leaders including Anthony Eden, Arthur Koestler, and President Roosevelt about the atrocities being committed by the Nazis on ethnic Poles and Jews. He was the first eyewitness to report to scads of people, the media, and religious and other leaders such as Felix Frankfurter, Cordell Hull, and others.

His big disappointment was the almost indifferent reactions he received from so many. One report said that when he spoke to FDR, the latter asked him about horses—not one question about the Holocaust.

After the War, he remained in the US and ended up earning a PhD from Georgetown, where he became a professor and taught for forty years. Until his death in 2000, he wrote many articles, movie scripts, and books. He was not afraid to express his views, one of which was that not nearly enough was done to help the Jews.

This was the man I recall visiting my mother in our apartment in New York. My mother was in awe. I remember listening intently to their conversation, although I probably did not understand a lot. I still remember his demeanor, shy and kindly but obviously uptight about his surroundings and history.

To a ten-year-old, he became an instant hero, as did so many who fought the Germans. I learned a bit about what our relatives must have gone through to survive the war. It also was one of the few glimpses I had of my mother's life at that time. Those resistance fighters and others who visited her presumably did so since she was the wife of a high-ranking Swiss government official. Switzerland, of course, was the leading neutral nation in World War II and often in a position to provide assistance.

The Swiss side of my family, not surprisingly, has never had much trouble tracing ancestry. Leave it to the meticulous Swiss (I often think I am more Polish than Swiss). It was not hard to learn family history, at least as far back as the mid-18th century. Tracing back to the 14th and 15th centuries has not uncovered too much, although word is that the original Nef came down to Switzerland around the 14th century from Norway or Scandinavia. He was a wandering and relatively impoverished farmer seeking a better life.

Family fame came several generations later, hitting a high point between about 1790 and 1830. A man named Johannes Jacob Zellweger, from the town of Trogen in the Canton of Appenzell, married Anna-Barbara Zellweger-Zuberbuhler and proceeded to have thirteen children with her. She died at the birth of the thirteenth.

Zellweger was an extraordinarily astute businessman, the first to do such things as import oranges and other fruits from sunny Italy to cold and snowy Switzerland. He also developed textile mills and lace factories. The products of all of these enterprises swept through Europe like a craze. The result was that Great Great Great Grandpa became Cantonal Governor and one of the richest, if not the richest, man in Switzerland. His fortune was at least partially lost during the Franco-Prussian war.

At one point while Napoleon was ravaging Europe, the emperor passed through Switzerland and took Great Great Great Grandpa as a hostage, probably in part because he was not only rich but also a political leader—governor of the Canton. Zellweger's capture ensured that the Swiss would not rise up against Napoleon. He was allowed to take one remembrance with him; he chose a small, hand-painted porcelain portrait of his wife. It now hangs on my wall in Alexandria. He was freed unharmed after several months.

Hanging in the closet in the family home in St. Gallen was the gown worn by Zellweger's wife when they attended the coronation of Napoleon. My third great-grandfather and the emperor evidently had become big buddies. In fact, in later years, Napoleon I's stepdaughter, Hortense (the daughter of famed Empress Josephine), was exiled to Arenenberg, Switzerland, near the village of Trogen,

Appenzell, where Zellweger resided. Prior to this, she had been made queen of Holland by Napoleon, as wife of another Napoleon.

Those two didn't get along, and apparently Hortense went off kicking and screaming. She hated the guy she was being forced to marry (who would be king). When she got there, she found she could pretty well ignore the fellow and enjoy life to its fullest. Hortense took a lover by whom she had a child. The pregnancy was skillfully hidden from view right up to the baby's birth. After the Napoleonic regime collapsed, she was forced to give up the throne and return to Paris, from whence she eventually was exiled to Switzerland.

In a letter dated September 2, 1977, my dad wrote me about Napoleon I's brother Louis Bonaparte and his wife, Hortense, and how they frequently visited Trogen and the Zellwegers.

He wrote, "You may recall her home, beautifully located on a hill overlooking Lake Constance. Hortense and her husband visited Trogen repeatedly. My Great Great Grandfather [Zellweger] entertained them always. Believe it or not, Zellweger fell in love with Hortense (by then Hortense was divorced). Being a widower, he wanted to marry her! But I understand that she declined, maybe because he had thirteen children, and she no doubt did not feel like having to take care of them. I only know that they did not get married after all, and Hortense died in Arenenberg."

My father wondered aloud about lots of things. At one point he wrote, "I often wonder about the value of the painting made by the artist Muller-Ury of me. Although the artist was not as well known as Hodler, still he painted not less than eight popes, their paintings being at the museum at Vatican City; also one of the German Kaiser Wilhelm." The portrait hangs in my office at home. At the time, my dad was in his fifties. I believe Muller-Ury painted the portrait for free. Apparently, he thought it good business to show off the important Swiss people he had painted!

At least four generations of the family shared the name Johannes Jacob. The eldest son of Jacob and Anna Barbara, also named Johannes Jacob Zellweger, a medical doctor and also Cantonal

Governor, married Anna Maria Zellweger. They had two daughters. One of the daughters married Johan Jacob Nef (1839–1906). Their eldest child was my grandfather, also Johann Jacob Nef (1865–1929). He married Rose Nef-Kern, my grandmother (1867–1954).

My great-grandfather on my grandmother's side, John Jacob Kern, was filled with wanderlust. As a young man in the 1820s or so, with five francs in his pocket, he took off with his brother for Mexico to seek gold and fame. He ended up spending close to twenty years there.

John's career started by working at whatever job he could get, the first as a stock clerk in a clothing store. I believe he was fired. John never made much money. He allegedly had a nice Mexican girlfriend named Rosa. Years later, back in Switzerland, he named his daughter Rose. A granddaughter also got the name. John and his brother moved to Mexico City, presumably to seek a better fortune but also to get away from the heat and humidity of coastal Mexico along the Gulf.

Finally, John Jacob Kern decided to return home. As the story went, he and his brother had cashed in big time at the gold mines near Mexico City. My great-grandfather would go first and bring the gold with him. Brother would close up the business and follow shortly. Alas, as John neared Veracruz, he was set upon by bandits who stole everything. He barely escaped with his life.

John then fell very sick; the tropics clearly were not good for his health. In fact, he tried to book passage on a ship returning to France, but the captain did not want to take him, doubting he would survive the passage. My great-grandfather pleaded with the man, who relented, but John had to promise no one would hold the Captain responsible if he died! I guess it was a tough trip—those were still the days of sailing vessels—but John made it. Sickly and dispirited, he returned to Switzerland to regain his health and well-being. His brother in Mexico never returned to Switzerland.

It wasn't long before the itch got John Jacob Kern again, only this time he was more rational. He lined up some good supporters; I imagine many were wealthy family members. Off he went to Paris. He married a nice Swiss girl, and he prospered, establishing himself in the family's traditional business, textiles and laces. I visited and photographed the home they had there.

They seemed to enjoy Paris. My grandmother lived many of her young years there, and it is thanks to that period in her life that she became fluent in French. She even preferred to speak it to her family and friends, which is the reason my father spoke French to me and my sister as we grew up. To the day my grandma died at age eighty-nine, in 1954, we always spoke French to her.

Hardships intruded again, this time brought about by world political convulsions. The Franco-Prussian War broke out, and Great Grandpa thought it best to send his family back to Switzerland. He would stay in Paris to protect the family business as long as he could.

Very difficult times ensued. There were stories that people in Paris were forced to catch and eat rats, for lack of food. Disease was rampant. When the war ended, my great-grandfather this time never fully recovered his health. But the family business prospered again under another generation, and it still existed when I went to Switzerland as a young boy.

My grandmother, a Kern, married a successful business man, a Nef—textiles again—who happened to be her first cousin. They had five children, all normal, thank goodness, despite the fairly close intermarriage. My father was the second born. It was the family plan that my father would follow in all these footsteps and join the firm for his career. Unfortunately, or fortunately, it was hard to pin him down (see a family trend?!), and he decided instead to join the Swiss diplomatic service. The rest is history.

As for the Mexican venture, in 1948 my father wanted us all to visit Latin America and try to re-establish contact with descendants (if any) of the brother who stayed behind. Our first stop was Mexico.

Mirabile dictu, he succeeded. We had a fascinating reunion with a branch of the family with which there had been no meaningful contact since the mid-1800s. It turned out that the whole tale of exploiting a gold mine and traveling to the seacoast to return home with all the gold was pure fabrication. They never found gold, and there was no hijacked mule train.

The brother remained in Mexico because he had no other choice.

The family in Switzerland today find the story amusing. They figure poor Grandpa was mortified that he had been gone for so long seeking his fortune and had come back sickly and impoverished, so he made up the story to satisfy curious relatives. Presumably he hoped they would not bother him with questions. It worked; it took close to a hundred years for the truth to come out.

I enthusiastically kept in close touch with my Swiss side, especially cousins close to my age. They all spoke English and liked to travel to the US, just as we loved travel to Europe and Switzerland. What's not to like? Skiing in the Alps in winter, hiking in the summer, wonderful food, family reunions, and travel around the rest of Europe and the Mediterranean.

Turning to more modern times, my dad became a bit of a Swiss personality thanks to the career he chose. When World War I ended, he was offered a position in the Swiss diplomatic service, which was just being formulated. His option was to accept that or to spend more time in the army in the post-war confusion. He also had fallen in love with my mother, who had come to Switzerland as young Polish student seeking a university degree. It doesn't take much guessing to figure out what he did.

When World War I broke out, my mother was suddenly stranded in Switzerland and nearly penniless. The Swiss people reacted generously to the challenge of large numbers of impoverished Polish students in Switzerland and opened their homes, taking them in as visitors for the duration. My grandmother had quite naturally immediately opened her home and offered to take one in, my mother as it turned out.

My mother had a hard time, mitigated by my very understanding and kind grandmother, who tucked her under her wing and gave her strong moral support. The problem was that my grandfather was very old-school. This was still the era of strong religious conflicts in Europe, Catholic versus Protestant, Martin Luther in

My parents in 1920.

Germany and Zwingli in Switzerland, which left deep emotional and psychological scars.

Even after World War II, when I first visited Switzerland, I was struck that deep cultural divisions still existed between Catholic and Protestant. I remember Protestant resentment that every Sunday, every Catholic church in town would ring its bells (and there were many) for fifteen minutes at 5 a.m. to awaken the faithful (and obviously the non-faithful). I am sure the Catholics found objectionable many Protestant activities.

My grandfather could not tolerate that my father would marry a non-Swiss *and* a Catholic to boot. As a result, they did not get married until a little while later, when my father joined the Diplomatic Service and was sent to New York City as his first post. My mother followed shortly thereafter, and they married in New York, ignoring Grandpa.

My grandfather essentially cut off communication with them, and it wasn't until a number of years later, when my father had achieved some success in his career, that relations thawed. A lot of that was thanks to my grandmother, who always kept the bonds close.

None of this impeded my father's career. Thanks to many factors —I like to think his competence, and well-meaning and friendly nature—Dad was rapidly promoted from lowly vice-consul to consul general in New York, one of the most important posts Switzerland had to offer. Several times he was about to be transferred, but something always interceded. As a result, his first post lasted twenty-five years, during which time my sister and I were born and grew up. His second position, as ambassador to Canada, lasted for fifteen years.

Both my parents thoroughly enjoyed Canada, and when Bern offered my father other posts, like Buenos Aires, Moscow and London, he always turned them down. They enjoyed life in Ottawa and had many friends there.

It turns out that my mother had dyskeratosis congenita, an undiagnosed and almost unknown inherited blood disease. She died of it. Most unfortunately, the blood disease appears to be transmitted through females, and my sister came down with it and also died from it at age sixty-four. In fact, this was the first time real attention was paid to dyskeratosis congenita only to discover that barely a handful of people seem to have knowingly contracted it through history. The medical profession finally took an interest and has been trying to find out more, spurred on by the discovery that her eldest daughter (my niece) also had it. My niece tragically passed at age fifty-nine.

None of our generation have attained any international fame. One uncle founded the first pediatric hospital in eastern Switzerland; another uncle became a well-known Swiss journalist and head of the Swiss Journalist Association. A cousin achieved recognition in the university world, and his sisters did much good work in the field of medicine. But no emperors or emperor consorts!

My brush with fame came from writing novels. Simon & Schuster made an offer on my first one, but my agent turned it down because he thought the offer was too low. Alas, no more offers followed.

I never did aspire to fame. As a boy, my greatest wish was to raise cattle on a western ranch. Sadly, my upbringing in New York City left few opportunities to practice animal husbandry. The city did afford other, wonderful opportunities, like Broadway shows, the World's Fair, and, of course, the rodeo at Madison Square Garden.

chapter four

Childhood Memories, Age 4–84 (Okay, 4–18)

We lived in New York City, but my father's job as Swiss consul general in the US required that we travel by ship to Europe every couple of years. My parents' love of travel meant that we also vacationed in different places, like Florida, the West, and New England. It was just something we did. I accepted it easily, recall enjoying it, and took it for granted. I pretty much accepted life as it came to me, probably not realizing that my American friends looked upon me as a bit different.

My friends would get a bit bemused when they came to my home to play and would hear English, French, and Polish being spoken. Or they might be offered foreign food and snacks. I never joined summer camps but instead would go off to Europe or elsewhere.

Friends seemed to forgive such digressions, probably thinking, "Oh, he's foreign, you know." After summer holidays when a friend would come back and describe a trip they had taken to Europe, I listened enthusiastically but was not particularly impressed. It was old stuff for me. But I believe that I was generally accepted by my classmates, and mostly I remember good times with them. None ever seemed to treat me differently. Being passably good at sports as we grew older probably helped!

Some American holidays highlighted our outsider status. Often it was a kid's thing that my parents would not even notice as being culturally important. Halloween was such an event. When all the kids went out trick-or-treating, there was no encouragement from anyone in the family to go out and join them. In fact, I was always a bit scared. Even in later years, I would stay indoors and let others answer the doorbell. The other kids must have thought I was really weird, but so be it!

When I became an American parent in my own right, I still wasn't enthusiastic. My wife would do most of the duties, although I did eventually enjoy trailing behind them on the street as they ran up to the homes and rang the doorbells. This could be a bit embarrassing. I remember joking with my kids before we went out, telling them I hoped they got lots of Nestle Crunch bars, since I really loved them. So what did Patti do in the excitement of the moment when she turned away from the neighbor's front door? She looked down into her bag of goodies and yelled to me with great happiness, "Hey, Dad! I got you some Crunch bars!!"

Valentine's Day was another US tradition not particularly known in Europe and so unknown to my parents.

My parents, bless them, frequently suffered in silence to make us happy. On one occasion, my parents had been given tickets to a baseball double-header, the NY Giants at the Polo Grounds. They accepted them so that I could see the event. It's hard to imagine anything could have bored them more than numerous hours of *two* baseball games in a row, but they took me and grinned with me through the whole event. I recall even getting a bit bored myself but dared not say anything.

Sports were of striking importance in most young Americans' lives, and I was no exception. I loved what school offered: football in the fall, basketball in the winter, and baseball in the spring. It's what most red-blooded American kids did. I did, too, but for me it was always a family struggle. I had European parents who did not understand.

In Switzerland, the government subsidized athletics as preparation for military service, but sports like soccer and others were run by private clubs not affiliated with schools. My European folks liked sports and other leisurely activities, but not to the great lengths experienced in the US. Here we were outfitted in uniforms and protective gear and reveled in comradeship.

"You want a *helmet* to play this sport? Please!"

My parents wanted to do the right thing, but they did not understand. They grudgingly accepted these norms. To me and friends, all the accoutrements were very important symbols of being part of it all. I loved walking home swinging my football helmet!

When we were a little older, our school sports would take us on field trips or to summer camps. This latter activity became a real obstacle in my self-identity. I'd come home and plead to be allowed to spend at least part of the summer competing in some distant camps or preparing for fall sports.

"No, no. Out of the question! Don't you prefer to stay with the family? We're all going to Spain, then visiting family in Switzerland. We'll also spend some time visiting historic places in Northern Italy."

That's the way family dialogues would go, and it made no impression on them when I would say that I would miss spring training.

"Spring training? What's that?"

Of course, their arguments made little impression on me.

Now, as I look back upon these family discussions, I realize that strenuous summer competition is indeed very American. My inability to participate certainly set me apart a bit from my American colleagues. What I did was different but character-forming and highly educational. Sadly, I still missed the togetherness that the physical and competitive development of sports provided.

By being a pest about it, I usually convinced my parents to relent and allow me to follow the all-American route, unless it took away from family activities. I had to concede the family alternative was never so bad, even if it kept me from my friends.

Despite such disputes, I could never doubt my parents' devotion to their children. In turn, my sister and I were very devoted to them. Hands down, the person who influenced me the most, probably without his even knowing it, was my father. He was a genuinely kindly, thoughtful, and very good-humored man. We always had fun with him.

A warm and loving father, he was also a bit aloof, not the type to engage in strenuous horseplay with his kids. He was meticulous and neat about himself. He always swam the breast stroke and kept his head above water, since he didn't want to get his hair wet and unruly. We used to tease him endlessly about that. And he always counted his stokes: "Well, I did 460 strokes today!" he would announce proudly. Sports like soccer, football, or any other contact sport were way out of his league.

I probably thought my dad could do no wrong, and I tried to imitate him. Even as a grown man, I wanted to follow in his diplomatic footsteps. I inherited his sense of adventure. He enjoyed tennis, swimming, skiing, and horseback riding, and we often did things together, especially as I grew older. He also loved flying.

It was thanks to him that I grew very fond of painting (our home bursts with lots of mediocre watercolors), and photography. I was still a child when my father taught me the rudiments of taking pictures, developing film, enlarging photos, using a darkroom, and so on. That hobby has stayed with me all my life.

When I was around age eight, in 1941, my parents took us to visit Washington, DC. The mode of transport they selected was the airplane. Commercial aviation already existed on a small, short-hop scale, like New York City-Washington DC, using the superliner of the day, the DC-3. My father wanted us to have that experience.

He had flown on the early postal service flights that were opening up the world to aviation, risks included. On one of those flights, my father's plane crashed, but no one was hurt. Later on, after becoming a pilot, I tried to imagine what might have happened. I surmised based on his report that in landing, the wing probably hit the ground, then the landing strut must have sheared off and spun the plane around with no further damage. These were flimsy bi-planes probably built largely of plywood. Somehow, that accident made him a true enthusiast.

With Dad and Irene in a row boat in
Thousand Islands, New York, around 1945.

One fine day, we all went out to the airport (I wore my child-sized goggles) and off we went into the wild blue yonder. The whole trip was totally uneventful, but was the thrill of a lifetime for me. It undoubtedly set me off on my passion for flying, which has stayed with me all through my life.

While Dad was my guiding star, I was also very devoted to my loving mom. She was more quiet and subdued, following my father wherever he went. She always showed her children enormous affection, but she could get pretty upset at her rambunctious son. Sometimes, when I was particularly out of line, she would fall back on her bed, pat her heart, and mumble something in Polish about not being able to take it.

When I was about twelve, I was returning from a friend's birthday party, for which my mom had dressed me in my Sunday best. A bunch of us were excited and started running through Central Park, chasing each other, tackling each other, and basically having a ball with little regard for torn clothing or grass stains. It was great, until we all trickled home. When my mother saw me standing in the doorway, suffice it to say she let me know how she felt about me in my new—now old—suit. It was a long time before she bought me another new suit.

My mom's inclination to revert to Polish when upset or angry with something I might have said or done helped me stay current with the language. With the passage of time and the inability through the war years to travel either to Switzerland or Poland, my fluency in French and Polish diminished, particularly Polish because of Poland's post-war isolation. But my mother, thank goodness, did her best to not let me forget entirely. I remember her very patiently making me read and speak Polish with her, even if only briefly at an elementary level, until I left home for boarding school.

I grew up quite accustomed to and relaxed about foreign languages. My sister and I spoke English together, I always heard Polish from my mother, and my father spoke French. As we grew older, he spoke more and more English to us (he was truly bi-lingual with English). My mother was not as gifted linguistically and always had a strong accent, but still she was conversant in English. My parents always spoke French to each other, and even a bit of Polish, which my father had learned, presumably during courtship. He was a gifted linguist and spoke six languages rather fluently. I suppose one could say we were a polyglot family.

French was a lot easier since we traveled to Europe quite regularly after the war, and my grandmother would speak to us only in French, as did the rest of the family. French was easy for them since it is a national language of Switzerland. Today my generation of family relatives in Europe tend to speak more English, reflecting how, with time, English has really become the common language of communication around the world.

But we still had to study languages in school. French was the main language, which was very easy for me. Sometimes I lost a little fluency with the passage of time and the lack of practice, but it would always come back when prompted in a classroom or when returning to a French-speaking country. The similarity of Romance languages made it easy for me to learn Spanish, which I soon spoke almost as fluently as French.

My childhood was undoubtedly enormously influenced by the biggest event of all in that entire period, the second World War. The US was not yet involved in the escalating conflicts abroad when I turned eight on October 20, 1941. My parents arranged a very nice birthday party for me; they allowed me to invite my little school chums to a party at the Swiss Pavilion at the New York World's Fair. There were about eight or nine of us. My father had been appointed Swiss High Commissioner and was responsible for the Swiss presence at the fair.

The 1939–40 New York World's Fair, which covered the 1,216 acres of Flushing Meadows-Corona Park, was the second-most expensive American world's fair of all time, exceeded only by St. Louis's Louisiana Purchase Exposition of 1904. Despite the imminence of war, thirty-three countries around the world participated in it, and more than forty-four million people attended its exhibits in two seasons. It was the first exposition based on the future, with an opening slogan of "Dawn of a New Day," and it allowed all visitors to take a look at "the world of tomorrow."

The US was at peace and was not going to allow the war to intrude. Hosting the world's fair was at that time a very important event, indicating participation in world activities. The whole thing was very exciting for me, and I remember running around the Swiss Pavilion, eating a delicious Swiss dinner, and even seeing a Swiss movie in the Pavilion's movie theater. The day finished with fireworks over the mall, a nightly occurrence. Exciting things for a little boy celebrating his birthday!

Less than two months later, we were at war. I will always remember returning on December 7 to our apartment from some day's outing. We entered the elevator and were greeted by the elevator man, who looked almost panic-stricken. He turned to my parents and asked: "Did you hear?" What, they asked. "We are at war," he blurted out. I don't recall much more of that evening. My parents were in some sort of shock, I suppose, and probably became engrossed in discussion, and we kids were left to our own devices.

Over the next days, everyone's world changed. My mother was probably one of the most deeply affected people in the neighborhood; her home country of Poland had been already been devastated by the Germans, followed by the Russians. She probably hoped and prayed that America's entry into the war would mean the eventual liberation of Poland. No one was cheering the sudden threat of open warfare and destruction.

Everything seemed relatively normal to a young kid in that immediate aftermath, although it was obvious that the adult world was changing dramatically. My mother huddled over the radio all the time, trying to catch the latest news, and my father stayed at the office until late every evening. We slipped into the routine of life in wartime, rationing food, gas, even candy. Troops suddenly appeared, everyone grim. My life remained relatively unchanged, up in the morning, rushing off to school, home in the afternoon, homework, early to bed. I suspect adults tried to keep children's lives steady and stable. So it went through the war years.

During the war, the major link for the Swiss between Europe and North America was the sea route running from New York to Europe. To this day, I remember one important event my father was involved in. The land-locked Swiss desperately needed a ship to bring food and material from abroad to Switzerland. As one can imagine, freighters were not in great supply. Finally, one was found, a beat-up old tub, but all that was available.

I went down to visit the ship with my father, and I remember how disappointed he was when he first saw it. But there was nothing to do. He ordered a huge Swiss cross to be painted on its sides, hoping enemy submarines would respect it. Amazingly, it survived and ended up being one of the principle deliverers of basic supplies to the homeland. The ship made the transatlantic journey, then the supplies were unloaded in Italy and transferred to trains to be carried to Switzerland after traversing much Nazi-occupied territory.

It was 1943, and the Swiss government, given the tensions and uncertainties of the war, thought it important that a Swiss official visit and inspect the Swiss consulates scattered around the US. My father, as consul general, was given the responsibility. He managed to include us in the travel, and we went by train from New York to Chicago, San Francisco, and Los Angeles, visiting key cities with Swiss consulates and relatively large Swiss populations and business interests.

We visited Hollywood, where we were thrilled to be given a tour of a major film being produced (*Buffalo Bill*) and meet with one of the big stars of the day, Maureen O'Hara. A Swiss costume director for 20th Century Fox introduced us.

Along the way, my father arranged some time off, and we took advantage of an invitation from a Swiss doctor who had retired to a large ranch in the White Mountains of Arizona.

Dr. Donnet had obviously been very successful. His retirement home was a huge ranch of several thousands of acres. He had rented a small, rustic cottage for us in a nearby village called Greer. This was 1943, and there was still a relatively underdeveloped atmosphere to the place, just a handful of people in the entire village area and surrounding lands. We were truly in the not-so-wild and very

*With film star Maureen O'Hara on a trip to
20th Century Fox studios in Hollywood, 1944.
The man on the left was the wardrobe director,
a Swiss national.*

appealing West. People still rode horses around or battered trucks. What more could a kid ask for?

What followed determined my decision that I would grow up to study agriculture and come back to be a rancher in this heaven-on-earth magical land. To make it even more irresistible, the Donnets gave us a dream vacation. They took us along as they saddled up horses and rode their range, checking on their herds of cattle and doing that what ranchers did. They had a foreman (I still remember his name, Ivan Pierce) who was a true-blue cowboy. He obviously appreciated what this meant to a young kid, and he was always going out of his way to wheel his horse around to point something or other out to us, as we rode exuberantly alongside.

One day they even rounded us up in their vehicles and drove us to nearby Mt. Baldy, the highest peak in the White Mountains. The good doctor had a couple of his cowboys take a horse for each of us to the base of the mountain, where we all saddled up and rode off, in total solitude, to conquer the peak. It was a beautiful ride across wild brooks and open fields until we reached the pinnacle, where we picnicked. As we walked around the top, we discovered it was littered with small shards of pottery, there as a result of Native American worship years earlier. I still have some of those pottery chips.

I must mention how happy I was and how fortunate I considered myself that my father had always been an enthusiastic horseback rider. He had taught us how to ride when we were very young. The ride didn't faze us and added to the excitement and allure of the whole venture.

One day we were all in Springerville to do some shopping. I stood outside the store waiting for everyone, since shopping didn't excite me. A big, open truck pulled up along the curb, and a young guy, sort of a roughneck, leaned over the edge of the truck and beckoned to me. The fellow leaned into the truck and brought up a little puppy dog on the end of a leash, sort of suspended by his neck.

"Hey, kid," he called to me, "Like dogs?"

Before I could answer, he swung the pup over the edge by the leash, then tossed the leash to me. "Here, you can have this one, kid." He chuckled, and then the truck lurched and they were gone, leaving me holding a dog on a battered leash. Good grief. What to do?

The family returned shortly after, and I can imagine their surprise when they saw me with a dog on a leash. The poor Donnets must have wandered what the heck had I done now. But they were very sweet as I explained (probably with tears in my eyes), and they immediately took charge and assured me they would find the dog's owner.

We bundled into our car and went back to the ranch. Irene and I were ecstatic with our new puppy, while the Donnets and my parents probably thought, *What a mess.*

The story ended happily, although during the night I remember everyone being kept awake by the pup which yelped all night long. The next day the Donnets announced that the true owners of the pup had been located, and they would reunite it with its family right away. Of course, Irene and I were disappointed. We saw ourselves returning to New York proud owners of a new pup, what my parents must have feared the most. How would we take a barely housebroken pup by train for three days from Arizona to New York City?

All this enchantment had to come to an end, and the day came when we bid the Donnets farewell and they took us back to Flagstaff for the return East. On the way, we stopped at the Grand Canyon and took a day-long muleback ride down to the bottom and back. Another memorable trip. I was so sad! The most fantastic time of my life was ending, but I had a renewed determination that ranching would be in my future.

Then and there I decided that I would attend agricultural school (I already selected Cornell) and return one day to the life of a rancher. This could easily be dismissed as the idle dream of a young boy taken by the romanticism of outdoor life in the West. But I had one big ally in this dream—my mother. She had told us as children about her childhood in Poland, where her family lived on a large farm in eastern Poland, which she loved very much. She really did grow up surrounded by farm animals and agricultural fields. I have to assume they lived the life of landed gentry, since my grandfather was of noble descent.

Our dog Daisy and me in Connecticut, 1945.

She always defended my plan and supported my ambition. Believe it or not, that passion stuck with me right up to the time I went to college. I had to make a hard choice, between the Ag school at Cornell or Harvard. I guess too much time had passed, and I made the choice consistent with what all eastern city-bred kids did. The dream had faded, probably to my dad's relief and maybe even a bit of my mother's. But all my life I genuinely have loved outdoor life and the freedom of country living, probably at least partially attributable to this early experience in the great and wonderful outdoors.

My love for the outdoors manifested itself most strongly when, some fifty years later, I grew enamored with Mongolia, its very sparse population, rugged and wild outdoors, strong ties to horses and other animals as a means for transportation, and real hardship conditions. Also, as I grew older, my wife and I bought a vacation home in a very rural part of Vermont where we still spend vacations. It is truly a lovely part of our country.

It became a part of family ritual that vacation equals travel for adventurous and energetic journeys. My father loved skiing, so from about age nine or ten I skied with my family in the winter, starting first in the hills and slopes of eastern Canada, then progressing to New England, Europe, or Canada. The love of the outdoors and the physical exertion were irresistible and bred into me. I am eternally grateful that my folks loved to do all such things *en famille*.

We also went on vacation to places where horseback riding was possible. Although my mother did not ride, she didn't mind sitting and reading a book while my father, my sister, and I found a stable where we could saddle up. During the war, when travel was curtailed and it was hard to do much, my parents found stables offering lessons in the country.

During summer vacations, my parents often rented a house in the Connecticut suburbs near beaches and country living. We all enjoyed the tennis, swimming, and hiking.

Traveling someplace, even not too far away in summer, always meant going somewhere different to do things that couldn't otherwise be done, and maybe learn new skills. My fondest memories involve some sort of travel.

My affinity for the outdoors probably was strengthened by the fact that I was born and raised in the Upper East Side of New York City and lived in the same apartment for all our years there. Our home was comfortable, with plenty of space for my parents' need to entertain diplomatic visitors. I attended an Episcopalian nursery and day school, Church of the Heavenly Rest Day School. None of us were of that faith, but I'm guessing the school had a good reputation for helping to raise sweet, innocent young kids.

I was of the era of "children should be seen, not heard." Sometimes, I'd be rambunctious anyway. I remember a Sunday dinner when I was about five, with a couple of my parents' friends as guests. Towards the end of the main course, I blurted out, "Did you see that?! Mr. X just ate two whole sausages and two helpings of potatoes!" After a moment's shocked silence everyone burst out laughing. My parents must have made all the appropriate light-hearted comments, as did the guest, and I was deathly quiet for the rest of the meal. For a long time, I was a bit shy around strangers. Even today, I'm not the best at small talk!

In kindergarten I met one of my oldest friends and, for a long time, a best friend, Oswald Johnston. He went by Johnnie, later John, and finally Ozzie, and lived just a few blocks away from me. I always wondered about him. How did it happen that every day when it was time to go home, a big, chauffeur-driven limo would pull up to the curb with his governess, and he would hop in to be driven home? The rest of us all walked, accompanied by an adult.

At Johnnie's birthday, I remember thinking he had a nice apartment—a Park Avenue duplex—but what struck me was that instead of his mother, it was his grandmother who presided. She was very nice, but decidedly elderly, and not the type to frolic on the floor with little children.

I must have mentioned this to my mother when I got home. She gave me a big, loving hug, and explained how sad it was that Johnny's mother had died when his younger brother, Robert, was born. So for the first time I became acquainted with death, and I vaguely recall being taken aback. Mothers stayed with children, or what would the kids do?

Johnny and I "graduated" from primary school, and both of us went to the Allen Stevenson School for Boys which went as high as grade nine. No longer a big shot as an older student in primary school, suddenly I was the new youngster in elementary school. It was good to have an old and trusted friend by my side.

These were important years, since we went from playing with building blocks to eventually having birthday parties where our parents would take us to Broadway shows, rodeos, and similar grown-up entertainment. We also grew more rambunctious. I'll never forget breaking the frame around a fine painting in Ozzie's home when I kicked a football down the main hallway of the apartment. Oh, my goodness! The horror. Fortunately for me, his family was very nice and never said anything to me. Ozzie only mentioned that he was advised to keep better control of his friends.

I always liked Ozzie's father, a very distinguished and successful senior partner at Simpson Thacher & Bartlett. He used to take us to Broadway shows and other cultural events in New York. Ozzie and I and other classmates would pile into the family limo. All the way to the theater or wherever we would make a huge racket pretending we were fighter pilots shooting the enemy through the open windows.

On one memorable occasion, an adult accompanying us leaned forward and told us he had a top military secret to tell us, but we had to promise not to tell anyone. "Wow! Yeah! We promise!"

He told us, "The US has developed a top secret silent machine-gun."

"Holy smokes! What an invention!" Down rolled the windows, our imaginary machine guns poked out, and our arms shook from the recoil of our weapons. Our lips trembled from the imaginary noise of our secret weapons, and our lethal airplane made it all the way to the theater in total silence.

My relatively easy, privileged life was occasionally disturbed by a hard knock or two. One afternoon when I was eight or nine, I was walking home alone as usual from Allen Stevenson when four young kids surrounded me and demanded my money. A hold-up at four o'clock in the afternoon! I told them I didn't have any, and gradually inched my way to the front entrance of our apartment, fortunately

I'm in the middle row, sixth from left, in
sixth grade at Allen-Stevenson School in
New York City, 1944.

very close by, then made a break for it. My parents were incensed and reported it to the police. Of course, nothing more happened.

Central Park, only a block away from our apartment, was quite nice, despite occasional youthful disturbances by street gangs. My friends and I managed to avoid these and stay out of serious trouble. One time a kid sneaked up behind me and stuck chewing gum in my hair. I went screaming after him, but he was faster. All I could do was go home and try to explain to my mother what happened. She was not totally and impartially on my side; I must have done something provocative, she hinted. For a number of days after I had a bald spot where the gum had been scissored out.

There also were a few most unhappy occasions when grown males would try to make advances. This caused panic for me. I really didn't understand; I just knew it was wrong. I would take flight to the protection of the maid or parent who happened to be accompanying me, or just run away as fast as I could.

It was my first introduction to this complex issue. As I grew older, I learned that this behavior among men was the exception rather than the rule. Also, bullying was bad no matter what motivated it, and one had to be prepared to fend for oneself and not be scared.

My parents always tried to make my life in New York fun and educational and made a big effort to introduce me to the arts. For example, I attended the opera (*Aida* was the first) and Broadway shows (*Annie Get Your Gun*, my first play with Ethel Merman, who was my first crush). The rodeo came every year to perform in Madison Square Garden. I loved that!

My sister, Irene, almost four years older, and I lived through the usual brother-sister bonding and fighting. During my younger years, we played together happily, especially during our frequent long car trips. Being the older one, she usually directed the play activities. I became quite proficient at playing dolls. Irene was very imaginative, and she devised all sorts of imaginary scenarios for us to play. It was like playing in a theatrical dream world. Maybe this explains why I always liked the theater and make-believe games.

As we moved into our more antagonistic period, Irene convinced me I was pretty dumb because I was born in October. "Smart people are all born in February—Lincoln, Washington, even Dad." And, of course, my sister.

I think some of that natural rivalry helped form a strong bond in later years. When she died at a relatively young age—sixty-four—it truly distressed me. She had been a great companion in our later years, and I grew very sympathetic to her. Her marriage was not successful but never dissolved, and her husband caused her much turmoil. All the while, evidence of her inevitably fatal blood disease was sadly beginning to manifest itself.

My worst memory from childhood is the terrible tragedy of a maid my parents hired in Switzerland, just before the war, to come and keep house for them in New York. Germaine seemed like a nice young woman. But as time passed, it was evident that she had some serious problems of melancholy and anger, mixed with moments of genuine kindness and loneliness.

There was apparently a romance that was not going well, and her family thought it might help her to be somewhere new. She stayed with us after the war broke out, since it became impossible for her to return to Switzerland. She grew sadder and sadder. My parents even arranged for her to have some counselling.

One bright Sunday morning in 1945 when I was twelve, she left the apartment for a walk. My parents grew anxious when she didn't return; then the phone rang. It was the police. Could someone come down to the district police office? Not knowing what to expect, my dad rushed down. He had been asked to identify a dead young woman who had jumped in front of a subway. It was Germaine.

All I remember was bursting into endless tears, my mother trying to console me, my father deeply disturbed. He had to go through the formalities and inquiries to notify all the necessary people. It was a horrible moment for me and the entire family as we tried to understand.

I don't remember much of the details, but I do remember the shock. I had always liked Germaine, even though I found her a bit difficult. I had never been close to any death, except the natural passing of relatives thousands of miles away, and now here was death not only up close, but violent and tragically young. How to explain it?

As I was young, and with parents who tried their best to help me recover from the news of a violent death, fairly soon life went back to something approaching normalcy. By then my father was already half-established in Ottawa in his new post as ambassador. He was setting up the new and first Swiss embassy in Canada, finding a building to occupy as a Swiss chancery, a home as an ambassadorial residency, and taking care of all the many details involved in setting up a new embassy.

My parents decided to keep the apartment in New York to allow me to finish grade nine, the last Allen-Stevenson offered. Perfect timing. Eventually, I was alone with my mother, who did the housework and all the cooking. She did not particularly enjoy that, and we ate what must have been pretty prosaic and routine meals, especially given food rationing and other limits. I remember lots of meatloaf, occasionally some potato pancakes (a touch of Poland!), but nothing exotic.

Of course, our diets changed whenever we visited relatives abroad, where we enjoyed Swiss sausages and meats, pastries, and vegetables prepared in more exotic ways. Grandmother's garden in Switzerland was filled with raspberry, strawberry, blackberry and gooseberry bushes, and she had plum trees, apple trees, and even a pear tree. It was always fun to climb those trees and pick and eat the fruit, or pick fresh berries off the bush.

My mother also was largely preoccupied by getting ready for the big move to Ottawa. It all came together rather nicely: the residence in Ottawa was ready for occupancy, the chancery opened its doors, and I finished at my New York school. My parents asked if I would like to go to school in Ottawa, but I vehemently rejected the idea. I was an American, and I hardly wanted to go to a Canadian school and leave all my friends!

I could start school in the fall of 1948 at Phillips Academy in Andover, Massachusetts, where some of my friends were also going. My sister by that time was already enrolled at McGill University in Montreal. My parents probably had a harder time seeing their boy leave home than I had leaving home for a life of greater independence.

Ozzie, as always, came with me. One of the big perks was being allowed to *smoke*! Boy, were we important when we lounged in front of the dining hall, the one place where smoking was allowed, slowly drawing on a "cig." We also got involved in sports—I grew very fond of playing lacrosse—and joined other extra-curricular activities.

Ozzie and I roomed together, but our different personalities began to distinguish themselves. Ozzie was much more studious (not hard, since I rarely enjoyed homework) and intellectually oriented, while I gravitated more to sports and communal activities. But we remained friends and, given our long history, he felt more like a brother than a friend.

It was around this time I had my first date, at age fifteen, and one of my first (of many!) regrets. Why didn't I give her a peck on the cheek when we said goodnight? I thought afterward that maybe she expected it. But what if I had and she had *not* expected it? Good grief!

I never liked school. It seemed silly to sit in a stupid classroom all day when there was a great outdoors so near. Fortunately, I overcame this distaste sufficiently to apply myself when necessary to get into college. Truth be known, they were probably more impressed by my various scholastic aptitude tests, where I always scored very well (nothing to study for those!), than by my classroom performance.

One of the reasons I hated school was undoubtedly my father's influence. Whenever he tried to cheer me up about going to school, he'd tell me how he also had hated school, probably thinking this made him a buddy in school misery. Unfortunately, his considerable influence caused me to think it was cool not to like school.

He would tell me how he had attended the local, Germanic-style schools of Switzerland, where teachers yelled and screamed, insisted on the strictest discipline under threat or practice of beating kids if they did not respond properly. Ah, Germanic discipline. Those were the tough old days at the turn of the twentieth century, which thankfully no longer existed. In hearing these stories, I suppose I had to admit that my school wasn't so bad.

Still, I can't say I enjoyed Andover: strict parietal rules, hard academic requirements, responsibility for oneself. On the other hand, I also made many good friends. I learned to enjoy some classes taught by excellent teachers, and the adventure of being responsible for my actions. I had no one to blame to if things didn't go the way I hoped. Significantly for my later life, I learned of Andover's emphasis on "*non sibi,*" the school motto, "not for oneself." We were impressed at Andover to be aware of the needs of others and help if we could. Looking back, I can see that I grew up at Andover.

Though we had been raised in a multicultural, multilingual family, my sister and I were thoroughly American. After McGill, Irene went to the Columbia School of Journalism and married an American. My parents were very proud of the two of us, and always boasted about their two American kids.

By this time, I had received training, mostly by osmosis, to be independent and self-sufficient. Ever since age fourteen, I had traveled the world, often alone, and gone to boarding school on my own. I think it made me self-confident about survival on the outside. I faced a world not to be feared.

chapter five

Defending My Country

Back in the good old days, we were blessed with at least a modicum of patriotism. We had just survived a horrendous world war and emerged victorious, proud of our accomplishments, and generally motivated by a sense of noblesse oblige. Even as a young boy not yet in my teens, I wondered what the chances were that I might be called up to serve. I daydreamed about volunteering.

Obviously, I was going to be heroic. I knew I would bravely fight off the Huns—Bam! Bam! Bam!—but I doubt I had any profound realization of what that meant. Certainly my possible death never entered the equation.

My father every now and then suggested that my Swiss citizenship (I had dual nationality, born of Swiss parents in the US) could be used to keep me out of the military. I categorically rejected the idea, and my folks quietly accepted my decision. Both my parents were profoundly pro-American.

We knew my father had to do what he had to do as a Swiss official; I fully accepted that, but it was not for me. I do not doubt that my father was sincere in his belief that the Swiss, by staying out of the war, and arming themselves to the teeth to defend themselves, did the right thing for themselves. The Swiss had adroitly, over numerous decades, established themselves as neutral in the European conflagrations of the era and that policy had served them well.

It is said that at one point during World War II Hitler actually contemplated attacking Switzerland, but he ultimately decided it would be too costly given the very high military preparedness of the Swiss. And what for? A country with very few natural resources, a rocky terrain, and a population of cheese-eaters and watchmakers.

The US had saved Europe, even though it stood in 1945 much destroyed, its infrastructure seriously damaged, its economy shattered. The losers were totally dispirited, and those who were friendly to the US (almost everyone in the Western world) were glad to take on the mantle of victors alongside us. We were amazingly good-natured and felt sorry for those Allies of ours who now had to face the monumental task of reconstruction.

We didn't try to take anyone over, including the Germans, and instead worked to bring back prosperity to the world. We gave generously to all, including the Germans. The only fly in the ointment was the Soviet Union. Many Americans hailed them as fellow victors, so it was a deep disappointment when fairly rapidly we found ourselves in a cold war with the Russians. The Berlin Wall was built by them totally to separate the two spheres of influence.

Despite the increasing well-being of the West, the Soviet-inspired separation grew, and we found ourselves isolated from countries we had long considered peaceful and friendly, such as Poland, Czechoslovakia, and the rest of eastern Europe.

One of the truly inspirational events was the famed Berlin airlift. The Soviets would not allow land transit to Berlin but could not stop air traffic. For months, the Allies mounted a non-stop airlifting of food and supplies to Berlin until the Soviets finally gave up. Meanwhile, we let dangle the other countries taken over by the Soviets. This was obviously enormously painful to my mother.

Thus the US found itself facing military challenges it had not anticipated. After the war many hoped that our modest military presence would be more-or-less benign—there to help rebuild the ravaged lands. Instead, the US military and its World War II Allies found themselves facing a threat from an ideologically very different enemy, one determined to overthrow capitalism wherever it existed. The US military hunkered down and took an armed defensive stance, which meant a long-term commitment of the US military to the defense of the Western world.

We couldn't look meek and mild; we had to protect the West. The Soviets had gobbled up all of eastern Europe, imposed its dictatorships on those unfortunate lands, and poured troops and armaments into the countries they had seized. This meant that we in turn had to build up our troops and expect a long tenure defending against Soviet encroachment.

So the US, which still had an Army manned by individuals drafted into service, stepped in and filled the void. All young men eligible for service were called upon to serve for two years in the military. The pressure was not too great. If you could show you were a student enrolled in a legitimate academic pursuit, you could defer for as long as you remained a student. It at least assured you of a four-year delay as you went to college.

We all pretty much forgot about it, at least for the next few years. When the war started, there was great patriotic zeal, with individuals rushing down to enlist. By my time, enlisting was viewed simply as a not-very-popular civic responsibility.

I had an opportunity to join the Navy ROTC program, and I was sorely tempted. Had I done an ROTC program, I would have gone to the Navy—maybe even Navy aviation—which meant four years. The only hitch was that the Navy ROTC was popular, so it required three years of active duty without any aviation add-on. Army ROTC, on the other hand, called for only two. That extra year did not appeal to me, so I waited it out as a draftee.

That was purely my decision, but I have regret about it to this day. It would have been great to be a Navy aviator. However, I have to admit that my two years in the Army had an enormous, positive effect on me. I would be very sad, in retrospect, to miss that unique experience. I'd be a different person, not necessarily for the better.

In the spring of 1951, as an eighteen-year-old Harvard freshman, I went down to the Selective Service office as required and duly signed up for the draft. At the same time, I claimed my student deferment, which was granted without any hesitation. Even though the Korean War was raging at that time, I didn't have to worry about being called up once the student deferment had been granted.

By the time we graduated four years later, Korea was winding down. The general lack of patriotic fervor was quite evident, and informal conversation revolved around how to keep a deferment. This resulted in a great growth of popularity for grad schools. I mildly disapproved; I thought we had a civic responsibility to serve. In Switzerland, all men had to serve in the military upon reaching eighteen, and I thought that was a good idea.

I was resigned to the fact that all good things come to an end, and my relatively carefree, not-too-arduous years at Harvard were to be a brief interlude before reality hit. Ozzie and I, of course, roomed together our freshman year in a big, old freshman dormitory called Matthews Hall. Harvard introduced me to whole new group of friends with different interests and preoccupations. Ozzie hung around with a more erudite, classics-oriented group, and I went the way of more socially-oriented or sporty friends.

At the end of freshman year, our diverging interests pulled us in different directions, he to Kirkland House, and I to Lowell House. Only on the rarest occasions would our paths cross, and that was the way it was for the next fifty years. Ozzie became a well-regarded journalist, working for various newspapers on the East Coast and the *Los Angeles Times*. We still get together now and then, and it always seems as if there has been no interruption in our friendship.

At Harvard, I majored in International Law and Relations in the field of Government, and enjoyed most of my courses. The famed McGeorge Bundy was one of my professors. I found him a bit pompous. On one occasion, when a rather controversial guest speaker was invited to speak, a bunch of us gathered outside the lecture hall to complain. You'd have to say that the majority of us were moderate Democrats. There were a few isolated conservatives in the student body, but no one paid them much heed, and they didn't make much noise.

Bundy, who had sponsored the speaker, stuck his head out the door and proceeded to chew us out for behaving so badly. Of course, we all turned away and went home without much fuss (after all, that was McGeorge Bundy telling us to behave), and the lecture proceeded without further interruption. Would Harvard's reputation have been sullied or enhanced had we been permitted to disrupt the lecture? I think sullied.

I also enjoyed the proximity of Radcliffe, the women's college, the ready availability of sports facilities, and the constant stream of extra-curricular activities. I joined the varsity lacrosse team and had a great time. It was a good life, and I did not miss Andover with its rules and regulations. Although Harvard was truly a wonderful environment in which to delay reality, it could not be delayed forever. If I have any regrets looking back, they are only that I did not avail myself more of the absolutely unique opportunities the college offered. I was perhaps too withdrawn and unwilling to project myself.

I graduated in 1955, but there was a period of uncertainty, not knowing when I would be called up by the draft. This was the fate of those who did not seek refuge in grad school. To await the big call, I went out and got a job with the Nestle Corporation in their US headquarters in White Plains, New York. A friend of my father's was a friend of the president of Nestle, and when he heard I was looking for a job, he called that man and asked if they could give me something short-term until I went into the Army. Presto, Nestle told me they had an internship program I could join.

In retrospect, I suppose it is a glaring example of privilege, but there wasn't much I could do about it, and I was happy for the job. I had been looking around in lots of places, but few potential employers were receptive. No one wanted to hire a person who very shortly would be whisked away to the military.

Nestle was very nice to give me a job, knowing it was just for a little while. It was real "intern" work, doing little local surveys, keeping in touch with local advertisers, and never rising to the level of any responsibility. But it was eye-opening and different from anything I had done before.

The bosses were thinking of a small local promotion where an individual could get a free ice cream scoop if he or she did something positive (I don't remember what). The bosses wondered what sort of a scoop would be preferable, so they set up a small board with five or six different scoops attached, and I had to go to the local shopping mall and ask passersby which they would prefer.

Most of the time, when a shopper saw me approach with my little display of ice cream scoops, she would turn and flee as quickly and unobtrusively as possible. The experience was ego-diminishing, frustrating, but character-building. I was a Harvard graduate! I learned the importance of a thick skin and of persistence. You can't give up just because the target tries to flee. There is a lesson in every experience. To this day, I am grateful to Nestle. I buy their chocolate whenever I can.

To accommodate my need to report for work in White Plains, New York, I rented the second-floor of the home of a nice lady in the suburbs. That, too, was an experience. She had a pet canary that she kept in my bathroom. I guess she didn't want it downstairs in her quarters, and I didn't mind the occasional bird squawks. But the bird was located on a table at the foot of my bathtub, with the result that birdseed was constantly spilling into the tub. Oh, well. I was young and undemanding, and the rent was cheap.

One fine day during my internship I received my letter stating, "Greetings! You have been selected . . . ," which was the way the Selective Service chose to tell you your time had come. I had to report for duty in September 1956.

I returned to my parents' home in Ottawa to pack my bag and prepare myself for going to war, should that happen. No one thought it would, but the possibility gave purpose to my stride when my folks drove me down to the border. From Ogdensburg, Canada, I caught a train to Syracuse, where I and several other morose-looking young men gathered by the railroad tracks.

My parents had waved me off, and both were embarrassingly out of control with their tears. Luckily, none of my fellow warriors-to-be witnessed that. My parents were born sentimentalists, and although they may have been a bit embarrassed, there was little they could do. The family was a crying family. My aunt in Switzerland was the

*My first day in the Army, Sept 6th, 1956. I am
the second one from the left in the third row.*

worst; dear old Tante Rose would start sniffling and tearing up as long as a week ahead of our departure back to the US.

Things moved rapidly after that. First, Syracuse, where we all filled out lots of paperwork and were duly sworn in. Then, back on a train and off to Fort Dix, New Jersey, our first contact with the real Army. There we all received buzz haircuts and were issued uniforms, clothing, and boots—the essentials. Lots of rushing around, sergeants yelling at us, sleeping in a barracks with some thirty other recruits in bunk beds. Obviously we were no longer at home.

I enjoyed forming first friendships. What nice guys rural Americans turned out to be. I was drafted in a part of the US mostly populated by farm folk and small-town people—northern New York, across the border from Ottawa, where my parents lived. Many had heavy rural accents. We happened to end up in the same basic training units, and we remained friends for a long time. We had fun in a weird sort of way—after all, we were being trained to be killers—and it made the whole experience much more palatable.

It was an odd mixture of people. Many of the guys had little more than a high school education and had worked much of their lives on a farm or in a rural environment. They probably had good cause to resent those of us who had gone to college and were more urban in our background. One of the things that really appealed to me was how they didn't display any resentment and accepted me for what I was. I in turn really went out of my way to enjoy their company.

They were fun. They had good senses of humor, usually quite colorful and a bit raunchy, but that was part of the fun. My education sure was broadened for the better.

We remained a very different and diverse bunch of people in our outfit, and that is what makes me prize so highly my military service. There was one of America's wealthiest individuals sitting alongside a person of very modest circumstances, peeling potatoes at 5 a.m., scrubbing pots at 7 p.m., walking guard duty together in the middle of the night, talking, joking, complaining in one voice.

We had in our company Mike Dow, the grandson of the founder of Dow Chemical, one of America's largest corporations. He became "one of us," always cheerful and modest, pitching in no matter how

lowly the task. The son of one of the largest manufacturers of auto-
mobile parts was a bit strange, but everyone forgave him, because
he approached his service with the same humble spirit as Mike. We
had a Yalie and several other eastern college graduates, but also a
fellow from a dirt-poor rural family, and another who was given a
choice between going into the Army or going to jail.

Mike Dow became one of my close friends, as did Raiford Long,
the son of a gas-station owner in Georgia. Raiford was a gentle and
entertaining person who made keen observations of our fellow men
in his slow Georgia drawl. We were a loose bunch of eight or ten guys
who regularly went off in pairs or groups to enjoy our surroundings.

We were all bound by an underlying common purpose: We were
there to be ready to defend the country, even though we never spoke
of that and rarely thought about it. I never would have had similar
experiences otherwise. I now feel sorry for colleagues who did not
get drafted. As I look back in my advancing years, this was the only
period where such an incredible experience was available to me.

At one point in advanced basic training, a whole group of new
recruits joined us from New York City, my place of birth. But these
guys were so different; they talked about time in jail, about times
so wild on the streets I wondered how they survived. My fellow
rural recruits and I stuck together and did our best to ignore the
newcomers. I tried to pretend I was a country boy, not one of those
woebegones from urban USA.

Time passed quickly and exhaustingly. I can't say it was easy,
but it was certainly a worthwhile experience. Awakened between 4
a.m. and 5 a.m., or even occasionally earlier, by a screaming sergeant,
dressed in a hurry, out to the mess hall to chow down, and out on
the parade field with our weapons (M-1 rifles). Then we might
march several miles to a designated training area, which could be a
huge firing range, to familiarize ourselves with all sorts of weapons,
from .45 caliber hand-weapons to submachine guns, hand grenades
etc. We also heard lectures on map reading, hand-to-hand combat,
and more.

I'll always remember bayonet training. "What's the spirit of the
bayonet?" a sergeant would yell. Then, thrusting forward with our

Army colleague Mike Dow and me skiing
in Switzerland on a weekend leave.

bayonet-equipped rifle, we would respond loudly in unison, "To kill!" I don't think it made any of us murderers, since we did think the drill monotonous and not inspirational.

Later on, I thought about our casual response to what the Army clearly considered important training. What if I had somehow found myself face to face with an enemy also armed with a bayonet? I guess I wouldn't have had much time to reflect on past training. Anyway, that's the way it went until, exhausted, we would be marched back to our barracks and dismissed for the evening.

This went on for some twelve weeks. After the initial few weeks, we were allowed off base for a weekend if we passed a rigorous inspection. That was nice, but a bit disappointing. None of us knew the Fort Knox, Kentucky, area (where we had been sent from Fort Dix for our training). I became friends with another recruit who dreamed to become a pilot. On one of our first weekends, he invited me to tag along as he went to the nearby rural airport to see the planes and talk to the locals.

This was fun for me, and *really* exciting when one of the pilots hanging around the hangar learned of our interest in flying and, seeing we were in uniform, invited us for a quick flight. Patriotism was still real, and we thought that was so nice of him. It was the first time I flew in a small plane, and it had an impact on me.

This was my introduction to the military. It had not been particularly pleasant. I had been compelled to do lots of things I never really contemplated doing, from cleaning latrines to peeling potatoes. Worst of all were the rigorous physical training, constant harassment by sergeants, little sleep, and playing war.

Basic training was over, and my next assignment came up: US Army Intelligence. Wow. I couldn't have been happier. So imagine my despair when a few days later I was told the assignment was cancelled and I would go to Advanced Infantry training. No explanation, just changed. I asked why but got no answer.

What did I do? Something I hated doing but saw no options, and I'm still embarrassed. I called my father, who, as Swiss ambassador to Canada, was a good friend of the US Army attaché in Ottawa.

Could he possibly find out why the change? This was particularly heart-breaking since I had already determined that the Foreign Service was to be my career. What chance would I have getting in if they found out, as they surely would, that I had been denied a job in the Army that required a security clearance?

My dad understood and said he would try to find out. Then a call came into the office at my base in the Army. I was being pulled out of Advanced Infantry and going to Fort Monmouth Signal Corps. They would go ahead and process my security clearance. No explanation. My company commander was rather miffed.

Apparently, the Army reacted positively to my father's inquiry and eventually came up with the explanation. In filling out the questionnaire for my security clearance, I had to list the names of family members living behind the Iron Curtain. I dutifully listed my mother's family. I should not have done that since I really did not know them, but I didn't give much thought to mentioning that connection. Well, I guess those who do clearances had a fit. They thought it would take forever to obtain information on all those relatives. Easier to just cancel the whole thing, which is what they did.

I had gone through several weeks of torment, wondering what was going to happen to me and my whole career path. I used tactics I didn't like, but I saw no other option, and it worked. It impressed upon me never to give up hope and keep trying to fix things as best you can.

Off I went to Signal School in Fort Monmouth, New Jersey, to learn how to repair telephones and repeater equipment. This was known as the country club of military training centers, since the studies were basically technical and obviously not physically stressful. In fact, there was a critical shortage of soldiers with such training (the Military Occupational Specialty: MOS, as the Army called it) and we were put into night school, which sounded pretty good to me. Reveille at 4 p.m., classes until 11 p.m., lights out at 1 a.m. for four months. It was close to New York City and many friends, with weekends usually free. What was there not to like, given the circumstances?

The day came when training ended, and we were about to embark on the real life of a soldier. Orders came down sending many of us, including me, to the 34th Signal Battalion in Stuttgart, Germany. We traveled by troopship to Europe. I recall the great unhappiness of most of my fellow GIs as we were crammed into holds filled with bunks three or four levels high. When the sea was rough, it really could be uncomfortable (I always grabbed a top bunk).

In Germany, we were part of the communications system of front line troops who were mostly infantrymen, tankers, machine-gunners, and others who would do the fighting and dying. All that meant was that for the while we would spend our days fixing telephone equipment. But, once again, fate intervened. As I checked into my new home, Company C of the 34th Signal Battalion, the receiving sergeant looked me over, then, after a moment's reflection, asked me if I could type.

"Yes, sir," I replied.

"Sorry," he said. "I'm going to have to put you in Headquarters Company to handle our financial clerk work." Like most students who went to college, I had learned to type after a fashion. We had to type our papers using hunt-and-peck methodology plus the pressure of time, which made most of us capable of typing reasonably fast and accurately.

The die was cast. Hallelujah! I would never see another telephone, and instead I would fill a slot in the Headquarters Company as a finance clerk. Obviously, it had precedence in terms of work assignments, since anybody could fix a phone—that was what we were trained to do—but no one had any experience in finance. Neither did I, but I learned rapidly. That's what I did for my one and a half remaining years of service. Very quickly I learned how lucky I was, since being in a Headquarters Company gave you much more freedom, less supervision, and a steady indoor job no matter how bad the weather.

Time passed rather pleasantly. Every now and then we still had to go out on maneuvers, but there was not much to do. We took our typewriters along, but there was nothing to type. Life in Germany was not bad at all. The Germans, for the most part, were reasonably friendly, although every now and then you'd come across a boisterous type who enjoyed telling how he had fought us in the trenches. But never do I recall that being done combatively or argumentatively.

Women were easy to meet and usually cheerful and friendly, although they would look us over very carefully before taking up a conversation. Most spoke some English, and I had taken some German lessons offered by the base.

Occasionally, work could get interesting. One day while on maneuvers the door to the quarters where we had been billeted burst open and a young second lieutenant ran in, pointed his finger at me, and said, "You have just been shot. Lie down and await evacuation."

I did as I was told, and a few moments later some troopers carrying a stretcher hurried in. The second lieutenant pointed at me, the troops grabbed my belongings, put me on the stretcher, and rushed me out the door to a field just behind our barracks location. They lifted me up very unceremoniously and shoved me in the door of a waiting helicopter. Several other troops were already in there, including some friends. Then, whishhhh! Off we soared.

A very short ride later, the helicopter flew over a big red cross—a field hospital—before settling to earth. Once again, the 'copter's door flew open, new troops grabbed my stretcher (with me obviously hanging on for dear life) and rushed into the hospital. A very serious nurse greeted us, and, after a quick glance at me, ordered that they take me into the emergency room. I was beginning to wonder how far they would go with this! I was placed on an operating table, and suddenly everyone disappeared.

I wasn't alone for long. The nurse and her stretcher bearers reappeared and proceeded to rush me out the door. "No, no! Stop. Take him out head first!" the nurse screamed. I guessed that taking someone out feet first meant they were dead. They took me to the hospital ward, where I was dumped on a bunk. I was handed sheets and told to remain near my bunk until further notice. There I was with a whole bunch of other troops who had gone through similar drills.

I rarely saw any more supervisors. We were on our own to find the hospital mess hall and free to pass the time any way we wished. Finally on the third day an officer appeared and told us to get our gear together and head back to our home barracks maybe thirty minutes' drive away. Maneuvers had ended. Trucks were buzzing around, and it was up to us to find one headed our way. We finally hitched a ride, and not too long after we were safe and sound in our home barracks. End of adventure.

In the following months, life was pretty routine. I had a good bunch of friends, and work was fairly leisurely, with plenty of leave time allowing frequent trips. My buddies and I visited most of Western Europe, from Scandinavia to Spain and Italy. My sister Irene, who was living and working in Madrid (her husband was the United Press International bureau correspondent there) invited me to Madrid for Christmas. Mike came with me, and it was a blast. I think my poor brother-in-law was happy when we finally left; you can take just so much Spanish wine and and GIs on vacation. On another such trip to Spain, my good buddy Raiford Long came along, and we had a great time, too.

Almost every weekend, especially when we could get a three-day pass, we took off for some ski or vacation resort. We tried to catch all the Grand Prix auto races, too. What made it particularly enjoyable was that I decided it was a good time to use money I had saved over the years to buy myself an Austin Healey sports car. It was light blue, convertible, low to the ground and with a nice growl to its exhaust. I figured that would be the best way to see Europe. Mike experienced the same inclinations and also bought an Austin Healey sports car. The two of us would regularly pile in a passenger and go off to some fascinating place or another.

The life of occupying US Forces could be nice. Gasoline was subsidized (twenty-five cents a gallon) by the government for its personnel, and all the big resorts had special luxury hotels reserved for US troops (two dollars a night). This was also a time when Europe, including Germany, was beginning to bask in new prosperity, and sports cars were very, very popular. A small amateur race track was near our barracks, and it was fun to engage in pick-up races on the circuit.

Particularly attractive were all the Grand Prix races around Europe. We regularly would roar off on weekends to go to Monza or

My boots sticking out of a stretcher as I was "evacuated" to the Army field hospital.

Lemans, or whatever Grand Prix race was not too far (which could mean a ten-hour drive) to admire our heroes like Juan Fangio, the world champion. A bit crazy, in retrospect.

My time in Germany began to wind down, and I counted the days until it was my turn to rotate out, get on a train to Bremerhaven, and sail home. As my troop ship made its way across the Atlantic to the US, something went very wrong. Suddenly, the ship began a big maneuver. It was making a 180 degree turn and heading back to Europe.

At that time, the Cold War was acting up. There were serious threats being tossed across the East-West border in Germany, and Lebanon had become a hot spot. There were about 1,500 troops on the ship, and none of us could believe what was happening. Our releases were surely being postponed and we were headed back to the East-West border to prepare for true military confrontation. Panic!

Thank goodness, it was a false alarm. Since our ship had medical services on board, all we were doing was going back about three hours to rendezvous with a civilian ship where a crew member had been badly injured in an accidental explosion on board. Our ship would give him the medical services he needed. We all breathed a collective sigh of relief.

After that scare, we had a stretch of rough seas for a day or two. I was rewarded for my apparent immunity to seasickness by getting assigned to latrine duty. This meant standing by the entrance to the latrine with a mop and having to clean the terrain whenever some poor seasick GI didn't make it to toilets. Ah, the joys of military discipline.

On the whole, I was probably one of the few who rather enjoyed the trip. I could spend most of the time on deck, watching the sea, curling up with a book, or just chatting with my congenial fellow troops. Time passed quickly. By August 13, 1958, I was once again a civilian.

When Mike Dow and I communicated again after fifty-nine years, he told me he considered his Army career one of the most valuable experiences of his life. Like me, Mike became interested in aviation. He ended up buying a rural airport in Michigan where he manufactured antique aircraft.

As we grew older, we both got interested in helping the less fortunate. Mike headed up a foundation operating under the Dow wing, while I set up my own family foundation. The only difference is that his is much larger than mine. That's okay. We obviously were raised properly in the Army.

I've said it before, and I'll keep on saying it. While I was in the service, I did not like it, and I grumbled interminably. But from the moment I got out, I looked back on the experience as one of the best of my life. In many ways, it made me grow up and accept my fate more philosophically. I learned a great deal about my country and about the fascinating mix of wonderful people who populate it. I learned how life is not so easy for many, and that has made me eternally sympathetic to the less fortunate.

I learned the importance of obedience, respect for authority, and to suck it up when things didn't go my way. These were all qualities, it turns out, I would need in abundance after I began my career in the US Foreign Service.

*A recent photo in my old,
old Army fatigues.*

chapter six

The Foreign Service

When I began college I did not have the foggiest idea what I wanted to do with my life. But I asked a lot of questions, and I observed different activities with the idea of finding a career path. The deck was a bit stacked, I have to admit. I had always been very fond of my father, even if he was a bit distant—not by personality, but by the demands of his career. His jobs kept him very busy, particularly during World War II and after, with limited time to spend with family. Still, I had an opportunity to observe a diplomatic career quite closely.

I remember well a visit from my parents when I was newly arrived at Harvard. They had come down to Cambridge from Ottawa, where my father was ambassador, to visit me. It might even have been for my birthday. It was a dreary day, and we were sort of stuck in my parents' room at the musty Continental Hotel. We were having a pleasant conversation about nothing, when I turned to my Dad and casually asked what he did in his job as a diplomat. What was his work day like?

He was very happy to tell me, and so I had my first glimpse at the functioning of a diplomatic mission. It dealt with bilateral problems; it protected its citizens abroad. It negotiated agreements on anything that needed attention at the moment. It complained when necessary and received complaints as well. It represented its country in everything from country fairs to international conferences. It entertained and was entertained.

I asked questions, and my father seemed delighted that I asked. He answered as accurately as he could, and his answers quite honestly made the career of a diplomat sound fascinating. It fit well with my background: child of a diplomat, world traveler by the time I was two years old, fluent in foreign languages. I felt very comfortable abroad.

I didn't realize it then, but the die was cast. My four years at Harvard had me majoring in international law and relations and travelling abroad on my own to such places as Mexico, where I picked up a fourth language, Spanish (and a love of things Hispanic). I ultimately decided to apply to the US State Department Foreign Service after I completed my military service.

That's when my problems with government bureaucracy began. It took me four tries to finally pass the tedious and lengthy (two days in that era) entrance exam, in part because each time they changed the format and the test requirements. In rummaging through old mail, I came across a letter I had written my folks in September 1954, wherein I described a bit about the test. I cited for them one of the questions:

"I had to write a letter to a certain businessman under these circumstances: I was with the embassy in a country with which it was important to have good relations, and which we were trying to impress with American freedoms, especially of speech. Now an American businessman comes along to deliver a speech in that country (which he submits to the embassy for clearance). However, that speech was very critical of country x's political and economic policies, and I have to refuse him clearance. It is also important not to alienate the businessman since he is important to the embassy. And I have to be careful that country doesn't take this as an example of freedom of speech. I then had to write the businessman refusing him clearance."

In another part of the test I had to list the major cities going up the Elbe River.

Then there was the little problem of my dual citizenship –American by birth, Swiss by heritage. I had to renounce my Swiss citizenship. I felt sorry for my dad, but he never said anything, leaving it up to me to decide. In fact, it was at his embassy that I did the deed. The need for such action was understandable, and I think my dad was proud that I was to be a US diplomat. Still, it must have been hard for him.

While waiting for the appointment, I went to George Washington University Law school in Washington, DC for a year. I was so thankful I had the Foreign Service waiting, and I didn't have to go into law as a career. Law was the pits for me. It was a tough time, since I couldn't wait to get started in the Foreign Service, and there I was learning the intricacies of real property law.

In retrospect, it was pretty shameful that the State Department was making hopeful applicants wait as long as one or two years just to see if they could get in. The reply to questions was a shrug of the shoulders and a short response: "Sorry. No money for new hires." So, with a former college classmate who was going through similar trials, I rented an apartment in DC for the interim while we attended law school.

Living in Washington was rather nice, with lots of young people and a lively social life. Most significantly, on a Valentine's day date, I met a beautiful young lady, Elizabeth Johansen from Westfield, New Jersey. Her cousin, who had a job working for the State Department testing division, set us up.

The fact that she was an American particularly thrilled me, since most of my post-college life had revolved around foreign countries and people. Finally I had a date with an American! She was the answer to my dreams. To make a long story short, six months later we were engaged, seven months later married, and ten months later on our way to our first foreign assignment.

This seemed like a natural progression for me, but I'm afraid I was insensitive to the total convulsion it caused my new wife! She took it like a real soldier, and soon she was leading a life I am sure she had never dreamed of ten months earlier.

Elizabeth was a small-town girl from New Jersey who had not spent much time traveling or going abroad. But she was always interested in international matters and admired her cousin for working at the State Department. During my years in the Foreign Service, she never complained and helped carry me through so many bizarre and very different foreign situations. She faced everything from eating strange foods to traversing trackless deserts, to wandering through dense jungles and crossing rivers filled with piranhas; it was certainly unlike anything she ever faced at home.

Finally the day came, and I was sworn in along with a lot of other people waiting for appointments. In about ten minutes, it was done. Hallelujah! Where did I want to go, they asked. Africa! I had visions of wild animals, jungles, native peoples, the break-up of colonial empires—pure excitement.

If you sought a specific job in a specific post, chances were not good for obvious reasons. But if you said you wanted to go to a large embassy in a large area, your chances were better. So I asked for assignment to Africa, a large area. Since I spoke French, chances were strong I'd go to a French-speaking post, of which there were many, and indeed that is what happened. I was assigned to Dakar, Senegal, on the tip of Africa's western coast.

Wild animals? Exciting native tribes? Go to East Africa. Peanut exports and a dying French colonial empire? That was Senegal. Dakar eventually developed into a rather cosmopolitan city, but in those early days it had a fairly long way to go to achieve any real sophistication. The culture was dominated by the French. There were at least half a dozen African dialects spoken, but everyone learned French, the national language. The schools were based on the French system.

Even the Africans seemed half French in character. The African political leader was a highly acclaimed French poet, Leopold Senghor, and the beautiful Senegalese women were slowly becoming

Liz's school portrait, 1953.

top-of-the-line French models. As a post, not so exciting, but I grew fond of Senegal and its people.

When Elizabeth and I landed at Yoff airport in Dakar at 2:30 a.m., the same arrival time for all international flights, we were very excited. It certainly was different: a warm and sultry climate, the smell of the ocean, and a big, tropical population center.

In the next few days, we were greeted warmly by embassy staff, who helped us get settled and fairly quickly found us a temporary apartment in the downtown area. There were plenty of shops and colorful local markets teeming with Africans and almost no Caucasian people.

Most working Africans lived in the Medina, or African quarters, which surrounded the center of the city. At the economic center, the Caucasian population dominated, but there did not seem to be deep racial tensions. As might be expected, affordability determined geographic divisions. There were many rich Africans in Senegal and some well-to-do suburban communities.

The European business community was there to represent large European (mostly French) enterprises, exporting food—huge amounts of peanuts and their derivatives—and African-made textiles and wood products. Business imported European food, manufactured products, tools, and just about everything a modern society would need. Most Africans were engaged in low-level storefronts and markets, selling local food products, baskets, and handmade tourist items. Wealthier Africans earned their living by integrating themselves into the French super-structure and representing the African side in negotiating exchanges between the two cultures.

Everything was quite open and not too many buildings had air conditioning. The climate consisted of two seasons: the rainy one, lasting from late spring to early fall, and the dry season the rest of the year.

The main problem in the rainy season was the humidity. The temperature did not vary that much over the year, hovering in the 80s most of the time. That meant endless mildew but also fantastic beaches and breezes and a languid tropical lifestyle. The unpleasant pests were year-round; I'll never forget on one of our first mornings in our temporary apartment strolling into the kitchen to find cockroaches the size of a large human thumb scurrying around. We soon learned it took a concerted year-round struggle to maintain the semblance of an upper hand over them.

Delicious French food was available at astronomical prices in grocery stores that pretty much imitated their parent stores in France. Seafood was abundant, fresh, and excellent. If one sought more perishable foods, like vegetables, imported fish, or fresh fruit, one only had to walk a few blocks to the African market. Individual salesmen also regularly stopped by the consulate to sell fresh produce. However, food had to be treated carefully as sanitation was not the best. Elizabeth had to adapt to the absence of a local Safeway for most of her purchases. She even ended up speaking and understanding French quite well; when she had arrived in Senegal, she hardly knew a word.

What bothered Elizabeth and me was the prevalence of leper beggars on the streets and sidewalks, pleading for donations while displaying their emaciated limbs. They would beg during the day, then retire to the nearby leper colony where limited housing and medical care was given them. Begging was their day job.

By far the most intense experience for Elizabeth in Senegal was giving birth to our first child. Especially notable was the near total absence of anesthesia. She had to grin and bear it. The technical medical service was okay, and the nursing care seemed okay. She was lucky that no problems arose.

I had a my own experience with the medical system when my hand got infected. The doctor and several assistants lay me on a bed, held me down, and then, Bam! The knife came down in the infection, split it open, and the doctor squeezed it hard to get all the infection out. A few stitches and it was over. No anesthesia. Go home now, they said. I was glad to do that.

One year, just before Christmas, every foreigner and/or Christian was stocking up for festive meals. A salesman came to the office door carrying a huge basket of delicious-looking oysters (shellfish were plentiful) at a wonderfully low price. I bought a basket, and that evening we enjoyed an excellent meal. The next morning when we left the apartment, we saw a big sign in French and Wolof (an African dialect): "Beware! Some oyster salesmen are selling their product very cheaply. Many of these oysters come from polluted beds. Do not buy!" Well, I guess we were very lucky. We felt fine all evening and the next day.

But what about the Foreign Service? Here is where true disillusionment began. The life I was leading was not the life my dad had described. I was not a consul general but the lowest man on the totem pole in a small and remote outpost. I had to read the newspapers and clip articles that I was sure no one read. I copied dry trade reports and sent them to Washington, where I was pretty sure no one read them either. Where were the glamor and the sophisticated, continental people? To sum up most of my assigned work—dull, dull, dull.

Looking back, it was pretty naïve to think otherwise. Disillusionment came because I never properly translated the ideal of diplomatic service into the reality that grunt work was required, and it would be done by the lowest-ranking.

Although we were aware of a large and sophisticated African and Caucasian population, our problem was that there were very few people near our age. The large merchandising stores and the big import-export enterprises preferred to train their personnel at home before sending them out to the colonies (generally considered hardship posts). So management consisted mostly of older types who already had experience. The older folk were always very nice to us, but it was not the same. We did become good friends with several American graduate students who also felt lonely.

The embassy showed compassion. When the local Pan American Airlines office was looking for American help, they offered Elizabeth the job, and the embassy approved it. Later, noting my wife's experience in office management prior to our marriage, and seeing what a rather lonely existence she was forced to lead, they bent the rules a bit and arranged for her take on a job at the embassy (in those days spouses were not supposed to work in the mission). That pleased Elizabeth—and me—greatly.

A problem for me was some of the staff of the consulate general,

With Liz at the Presidential Ball in Dakar, 1960.

which became an embassy after about a year, when French President Charles De Gaulle granted independence to most of France's colonies in Africa. My boss was the head of the economic section. He was a Lebanese naturalized citizen, and his wife was Egyptian. Both spoke English with marked accents. Although they were not the sophisticated diplomats I had expected, they were both nice to my wife and me, and I didn't mind him as a boss.

The wife unfortunately had a huge reputation for being very difficult with everyone, which I never observed directly. The problem was that he and the head of the political section, Pierre Graham, were in considerable conflict personality-wise. My boss once even arranged a whole diplomatic party for the sole purpose of *not* inviting the other one.

Pierre was the one man on the staff I thought actually did meet the profile of a good diplomat. He ended up being my informal mentor. I owed him a lot for keeping me sane, and he went out of his way to help me in my career. His wife, a beautiful German, was the talk of the town.

The general services officer somehow had become a Foreign Service officer and managed to receive a foreign assignment. Although of low rank (that of a young beginner), he was considerably older than just about everyone in the Foreign Service with the same rank. He was American but not schooled in diplomacy. He also was incredibly lazy and inefficient. If you ever wanted something fast from his section, good luck.

I resented a bit that I would compete for promotions with people trained in management skills, not diplomacy. It didn't seem fair to either specialty, but that is what the powers decreed, and we all had to live with it. In an effort to promote specialization in what they called the administrative cone, anyone with any administrative skills was pushed ahead and given rank and title as a reward. Too bad for the economic and political majors who thought dealing with economic and political issues is what diplomacy was all about. If you wanted rapid promotion, better to know how to clear things through customs quickly.

My working colleagues were all much older and thus not natural peers. There were many foreign-born individuals running the US mission—not only on the officer side, but particularly on the distaff side. This was probably not intentional. Maybe foreign-born and -raised American citizens were not as fussy as native-born, were more agile with foreign languages, and more used to what Americans might consider hardship posts. My wife was one of just two wives who were American-born. The others were French, German, Egyptian, Russian, Italian or whatever.

There was a fair amount of petty back-biting and gossiping among the staff, with little cordiality among them. It made for an unhappy atmosphere. Perhaps most shocking to me (I was very young and innocent) was the promiscuity going on at all levels in the office. I even heard that my mentor, the political chief, and his wife took part. I did not think that was acceptable, but there it was.

I might add, in defense of the Foreign Service, that these antics seemed somewhat unique to Senegal's post. Other posts probably were not pristine, but at least not so openly bacchanalian. It must have been the cool ocean breezes, the warm, lazy tropical days, the French atmosphere of fine food and wines. And maybe it was not as bad as I, in my innocence, imagined.

We actually made good friends with some of the non-diplomatic staff. There was an American contracting officer supervising the construction of a new residence for the ambassador; also, the administrative assistant to the ambassador. The latter joined us occasionally on our trips into the back country. Once, we visited a tribe that allegedly still practiced cannibalism, only to have the head of the tribe offer to buy the administrative assistant from us. There was also a delightful administrative assistant and his French wife; we had so much fun with them.

There were also the occasional outsiders, like a fellow working on his doctorate and his wife. They were a delightful couple and one of the very few anywhere close to us in age. Our entertainment consisted mostly of doing family-to-family things, going on picnics, meeting at the beach, brief trips to the interior, parties at home (endless charades). But talk about beaches . . . the entire coast for miles going either north or south was nothing but vast expanses of beach.

There were other people, too, who helped make the tour enjoyable as long as it didn't involve the office. Very fortunately for me, among the staff who arrived in Dakar following President Kennedy's victory was the director of a newly established AID mission, Jack Vaughn. We became good friends despite differences in rank and age. I even took him by plane on trips to remote interior locations. It was lots of fun; in fact, I began to wonder if maybe foreign aid was a better career path than State Department diplomacy.

When the consulate was converted into an embassy after Senegal became independent, there was a marked improvement in the senior staff. Phil Kaiser, a political appointee from the Kennedy administration, arrived to serve as ambassador, and things got better. I even tried to extend my stay. The political officer and I were to be assigned to Nouakchott, Mauritania, to open an embassy there, and my wife was to be the administrative officer. To my considerable disappointment (disappointments appeared much too often), the government never got its act together to create an embassy compound in time for anyone to go up there. Instead, it was back to Washington after a little more than two years in Senegal.

An onward assignment to Alexandria, Egypt, never had a chance to materialize, and then was changed to an assignment in language training. I was to learn four African languages for future assignment to central Africa. What happened next was a quirk of fate.

One day after we had returned to Washington, where I would wait for my onward assignment, I was having a coffee in a local Hot Shoppe and bumped into Jack Vaughn. He, too, was back in Washington and working as regional director for Latin America at the Peace Corps. We greeted each other heartily, after which he asked if I would be interested in taking a leave from State and joining him at the Peace Corps to work as a program officer in Latin America.

Without hesitation, I eagerly accepted, never wondering what the Foreign Service establishment would think of this young feller so new to the service already accepting an inter-agency assignment.

I was also motivated by my great admiration for Jack; he was far from being a government bureaucrat—dynamic, inquisitive, and always open to new ideas. It was no wonder Sargent Shriver hired him, and that Jack fit in so well with the New Frontier and the Kennedy mystique.

Go I did, and I loved it. The newly formed Peace Corps, under a dynamic Kennedy family member, Shriver, was open to just about anything. Wow, was it exciting! I spent two years, from 1962 to 1964, traveling in Latin America, developing volunteer programs in remote corners of distant lands—so fulfilling. One could see the immediate results of one's work, as volunteers began streaming overseas to carry out programs I and others had developed under a great boss.

The Peace Corps was the direct opposite of my embassy engagement in Dakar. In some respects, my boss was a person I considered a genuine friend. Individuals were given tasks and then told to do them. And best of all, for so much of the work I was on my own, in the great outdoors, meeting people from many walks of life and from very different backgrounds.

Most of my travel was in Central America. As an undergraduate, I had taken a summer course in Mexico where I first learned my Spanish and grew fond of the region. I thought it nice to return to speaking Spanish, which came back to me quickly, and it was invigorating to branch out to a new region. Each of the small Central American republics was very different, and future volunteers would face different situations and problems depending on where they would be assigned.

I remember being on horseback in the rural and isolated countryside, my companions a couple of native *campesinos* and a local teacher. We were headed to a remote farming community to see if it would be appropriate to send a Peace Corps volunteer to work there for close to two years. We spent the night with our new friends in a very primitive home with thatched roof and central fireplace. It was so exciting and, well, different. We met with the local "authorities" and other local leaders, then returned to our office and residences in the capital city to report findings, and ultimately make a decision on the project.

Then it was off to another site, perhaps a fishing village. After the various explorations and decisions, we flew back to headquarters in Washington to write up reports and recommendations and await prompt assignment to perhaps another country, or another subject. I remember thinking to myself, "Wow! Am I really getting paid to do this?"

Also, one easily became involved in other aspects of running the agency. One could be called upon to go out on extensive two-week trips to various parts of America to recruit new volunteers. This consisted mostly of travel to college campuses, meeting with great numbers of students, and even administrators, to tell them about the Peace Corps. We described what it meant to be a volunteer, what they could do, and how popular volunteers were in local communities. The applications poured in.

My poor wife, a new mother to our daughter Christine, was not too happy. My new job required a great deal of travel, either overseas on program development or in the US on recruiting and management matters. Time spent at home was always being squeezed. We didn't dare mind too much, because that was the gung-ho spirit of the Peace Corps.

It was great to work with an entirely different cadre of people— no more State Department bureaucrats. But these had their quirks, too. Ambitions lay in very different directions, no longer the bureaucratic climb up the career ladder. Shriver had installed an unusual policy: No one was to work with the Peace Corps longer than five years. That meant staff always had to be on the look-out for their future livelihood; it created a very different atmosphere. Also, since the Peace Corps was a highly political agency, with the president's brother-in-law running the place, there was a tendency of individuals to always be looking at the political angle of their employment.

The age of my new colleagues was generally younger than in the State Department. I was always young-looking for my age, and one day Shriver saw me and Jack together. Jack told me later that Shriver had enjoyed teasing Jack about his staff "Kiddie Corps." Maybe someone had teased Shriver about how young an agency he was establishing.

For me, the mix of Americans coming into the organization was refreshing—so different from the Foreign Service. One could easily be dealing one moment with young American farmers, the next with trained auto mechanics, all wanting to contribute to the cause. The one big fly in the ointment, it must be reported, was that most young people volunteering were liberal arts majors with scant practical skills. Before sending them overseas, much effort had to be spent training them in at least the rudiments of a practical skill, not an easy thing to do.

Such problems ended up being a big drawback, and some programs lost more than half their volunteers for their failure to become technically useful in a developing world. This was a problem that continued to plague the Peace Corps through the early years and beyond. The volunteer of today is quite different from the volunteer of the 1960s—more highly trained and experienced than in the early days, when volunteers were often barely out of college. Also, more volunteers with work experience began to apply, and older volunteers as well—recently retired folks out for an adventure.

My stint with the Peace Corps was the most fun I had during my foreign service career. The two years passed too rapidly before it was time to go back to the State Department. Shriver offered me another job in inspection and evaluation of Peace Corps programs if I would stay on. After much thought, I declined. I needed to give State another chance, I told him, and not condemn it on the basis of one tour. I didn't tell him I also worried a bit about being away from State so long. What would they say over there?

I learned that my successful record in the Peace Corps carried little weight in the Foreign Service. There were no detailed analytical reports of obscure events of little interest to anyone. Instead, I had zoomed around Latin America under the influence of the Kennedys in a program that State considered of marginal value to US diplomatic interests.

So back I went to State, unsure of my prospects. Thanks to Pierre Graham, my old political chief friend in Dakar who by then headed a division of personnel, I landed a fine assignment as a political officer in Guatemala in 1967.

There was a brief interlude while waiting for the assignment to come through, and I was assigned to the Uruguay desk. They were swamped with a regional issue of considerable concern: Uruguayan Communists had begun kidnapping people as a way to scare them and raise funds through ransom. This had worked well for the Communists until they chose to kidnap an American. The embassy quickly made the point that we did not pay ransom, and thus developed a rather dangerous standoff. I worked on this problem over a number of weeks, which consisted mostly of passing threatening messages back and forth. Eventually, it was successfully resolved through negotiation.

———

The situation in Guatemala fascinated me. An active Communist guerrilla band operated in the back country, and as the junior officer it was my job to "cover" them. This meant I was to report on their activities and, if possible, even establish some contact with them. I got to know some of them, and I found that for the most part they were leftist youth (none identified themselves as Communists). Some young supporters were not particularly politically indoctrinated but liked the adventure of challenging the status quo. These were the ones I was able to deal with most easily, and they had no problem talking to an embassy officer.

There also was a leftist political party that the Guatemalan establishment identified as quasi-Communist, but it was allowed to function openly, because most neutral foreigners and moderate Guatemalans did not think it was all that bad. Its leader, Villagran Kramer, espoused such radical (for Guatemalans) programs like social security and retirement benefits. I got to know him quite well; in fact, we sort of became friends.

It took a lot of courage on his part to take the stands Kramer did in Guatemala, but the arch-conservative Guatemalans knew that he had friends in the foreign community and dared not be too aggressive against him. For example, after much debate, the

Being sworn in after a promotion in Guatemala.
Ambassador John Gordon Mein (on the far left)
who swore us all in was assassinated a few months
later by the Guatemalan Communist guerrillas.

embassy approved my hosting a reception where Kramer would be a guest. Of course, he jumped at it, and reveled in all the looks he got from Guatemalans at the party. What was *he* doing at an American reception?

In one incident, there was an attack on the local jail to spring the leader of one of the most radical groups. As he fled in search of his getaway car, he ran through several backyards, including ours. My wife and I were out. He went on to the house of a fellow officer, and burst upon their maid, who was making the beds. Waving a gun, he yelled at her to show him how to get out. Terrified, she pointed to a door and out he went, passing through their children's room, where the children were playing, and was gone. Out on the street again, he found his getaway car, and in the blink of an eye, the car roared off. They got away before the police arrived.

Another similar incident occurred nearby a few weeks later, when the guerrillas attempted to assassinate the local police chief. He was one tough guy; when they cut him off in his car, he quick-wittedly slammed on his brakes and leapt from his car, drawing his weapon as he did. Flinging open his car door and crouching behind it, he blazed away at his attackers, who turned and fled. I guess that wasn't what they expected!

Guatemala was becoming more and more dangerous. The belligerents became radicalized. At first, they had been a motley crew, lots of young people out for adventure. But more and more Communist ideology was taking root, and violence was a distinct part of their strategy. Shortly after we left on transfer to our next post, they ended up assassinating our ambassador and several others.

I did a good enough job in my role as political officer that on several occasions, individuals with the CIA let it be known that I would be well-received if I jumped ship and went to work for them. At that time, the CIA was the glamorous agency, and many of my fellow junior Foreign Service officers thought about it. By and large, most seemed content to remain with State. Only one of my close friends transferred, and it did not take too much time before he disappeared from my view.

I also had a mindset which told me that career would be unwise. I genuinely was concerned that my Polish background would disqualify me. The CIA would fear I would be targeted for subversion. True? I don't know, but I feared it. I know it took a *long* time for the State Department to give me my security clearance. They told me this was simply a bureaucratic issue, given my many relatives behind the Iron Curtain. If it took State a long time, I could imagine how the CIA would handle the issue.

Still, the CIA did tempt me at that time of my life. There were certainly many positive aspects. One very positive influence was the number two CIA person at the embassy in Guatemala, Dick Welch. He was just a couple of years older than I and doing very well in the agency. We became good friends because we had shared interests and similar educational backgrounds. He was only a couple of years ahead of me at Harvard, and we both played tennis and enjoyed adventure.

He was a genuinely nice person. He let me in on some of the dirt the CIA had picked up, and I offered him a bit of cover when we travelled together in the back country. I always had my official diplomatic passport justifying my journeys; he, too, had one, but it was one that made him look like some minor person. I remember he gave us a very nice farewell party when we left Guatemala.

Dick invited me once to dine with him in the inner sanctum dining hall of the agency in Langley Park. I still recall with some amusement that meal; we walked through the halls, and I noted no door had any names and no one wore name badges. Spook city, I guess.

I was stationed in Washington when on the front page of all the newspapers was the news that the CIA station chief in Athens, Greece, Richard Welch, had been assassinated as he returned home with his wife. Apparently, as he had climbed out of his car, a man had walked up to him and shot him point-blank in the head.

A while later I received an invitation from top brass at the agency to attend a memorial reception in Dick Welch's honor. The function was attended almost exclusively by CIA personnel; I'll never know how my name ended up on the list. What surprised me was seeing a number of people whom I thought I knew as State Department employees. They looked just as surprised seeing me as I was seeing them.

At that time in Guatemala, despite the appeal of the CIA, I was not sure I would have liked going into truly clandestine work. The thought of living a secret life and having to deal with unsavory people willing to sell their country for cash was not appealing to me. I recognized the need for this, but that did not mean I wanted to do it. Had I known what the State Department had in store for me, I might have changed my mind!

I liked the country team in Guatemala: good people, challenging work, and many fine friendships. I hoped for a good onward assignment after Guatemala, and my bosses—first Richard Dreyfuss and then Matt Smith—who epitomized great bosses, tried very hard to promote me.

Alas, that was the year the State Department decreed that very few promotions would go to traditional political and economic officers. The ones to be promoted were administrative officers. It did not matter how good your political work was; what mattered was whether you could get things through customs rapidly and pay bills promptly. For me, it was shocking. *That* was diplomacy?

No promotion for me, and instead sort of a demotion in 1968, from number two in the political section in Guatemala to number three in the much larger embassy in Bogotá, Colombia. It was very different from Guatemala, very formal, with men dressed in black suits. On a plateau some 9,000 feet above sea level, Bogotá had year-round cool weather and quite a bit of rain.

The political scene was quiet, especially compared to Guatemala. This was thanks to incredible wisdom on the part of the Colombians. They had suffered a period of enormous violence, murder, and political instability, when finally all the leaders on all sides of the spectrum declared that could not go on. They sat down together and negotiated an agreement to bring peace: First one party would control the country; after four years, they would hand over the reins to the other party for four years, and so on. Believe it or not, it worked. It brought peace and lasted for a number of years.

It didn't take long to find that Guatemala had been a unique experience. First, the embassy in Bogotá was very large—much larger than in Guatemala—and no one seemed very friendly. The staff were highly compartmentalized, and nobody seemed to care what was going on. Worst of all, I soon learned that my boss, the head of the political section, was an alcoholic.

I'll never forget one of the first receptions I attended at the home of the economic counselor, a very fine residence with a small interior fish pond. At some point in the evening, I heard a loud splash. To my horror, I saw that my boss had drunkenly fallen face first into the pond. I helped fish him out while guests looked on.

Eventually he was transferred out and a new political counselor came in who made me long for the alcoholic. This one was out of his depth and not very nice. I couldn't help but wonder how he ever made it to that level.

One of my former bosses in Guatemala had actually been transferred to Guatemala from Bogotá. He was excited to hear of my transfer there and thought it a good post. Before leaving, he gave me a list of his best contacts in the Colombian government and urged me to look them up. When I showed the list to the new boss, he took one look at it and declared they were all too high-ranking for me to deal with. If I wanted, he said, I could try to establish contacts with the secretaries of these men. "You can learn a lot from the secretaries," he told me.

He loved to travel around the country with his camera like a tourist. This was a front for him to take photos, which I would then identify and send to the intelligence bureau—"They want that sort of stuff," he said. Actually, they were all pretty much typical tourist pictures, but this way the department would pay for his film and its processing, which is what he wanted.

The other political officer and I commiserated constantly, played lots of chess, and decided there was little to do other than wait, since we agreed our boss was a hopeless disaster. I'm sure I could have tried harder; there were good people in the embassy, and I could have sought them out. We had many good friends and had some enjoyable times together. But really, I was in despair and waiting for a chance to get out. I knew such action would be very bad for my career, but I didn't care.

Looking back, this time in Bogotá was the most difficult period of my life. I was sort of lost in an embassy where I found few sympathetic colleagues. The guidance and support we needed to do the job we were supposed to do was nonexistent. No one showed any interest in my work.

I was driven to distraction when one day the embassy was visited by my friend Jack Vaughn, the former head of the AID mission in Dakar and sponsor of my first tour with the Peace Corps. He had been promoted to director of the Peace Corps after Kennedy's assassination and Shriver's departure to head the government's anti-poverty program.

I grabbed an opportunity to see him briefly and laid it out. I told him how miserable I was, and would it be at all possible to have another assignment with the Peace Corps? As usual, he was so gracious and listened with an attentive ear. We parted with a firm handshake.

Not too many days later, I learned that I was to return to the US and be assigned as director of International Multi-lateral Programs at the Peace Corps, which meant providing liaison with all the similar programs that had sprung up around the world. This included the United Nations, which was talking about creating a UN Volunteer Corps. I counted my blessings. I left Bogotá in 1969, fewer than two years after arriving—not a good career move—but I didn't care.

Then, a strange twist of fate. Not too long after, Jack was appointed ambassador to Colombia, which meant my mentor and supporter was gone. Instead, President Nixon appointed a young Republican, Joe Blatchford, as the new director. Nobody knew him. Again, I feared for my professional life. Once again fate intervened: it turned out that Nixon favored multi-lateralizing many programs, including volunteer work. I convinced my new boss that there was a great opportunity for him if Nixon gave the Peace Corps credit for helping create a UN Volunteer Corps, and my office was the one to handle that. He liked the idea, and I was off to the races.

Talk of an international volunteer corps had already been kicked around, but up to that point no one had proposed it on such a big scale as the UN. Some smaller and private volunteer organizations were certainly using volunteers from more than one country. But the concept needed an international host to be successful; nationalism was too strong to allow one nation to assume any sort of international cover. The UN was kicking the idea around but was somewhat adrift with little or no experience in volunteer programs. We were ideally situated to help them, and they bought the idea.

The next year was spent working closely with the UN to do exactly that—help them create a UN Volunteer Corps. All this was very challenging for me. I had never done anything like it, never been so independent yet part of an organization I respected greatly.

The UN had little experience in this type of volunteer work, nor what it needed to do to accomplish that objective. I ended up working very closely with them and helped them create the framework for a UN volunteer Corps. They were good and hard-working people but did not have backgrounds in volunteer organizations. The program ended up resembling the structure and objectives of the Peace Corps, except volunteers it recruited and trained would work under UN management. It remains a part of the UN structure to this day.

Joe Blatchford, the new head of the Peace Corps, was very happy when I delivered the UN's executive document to him. From having been standoffish with me, Blatchford suddenly became a big buddy, especially when Nixon reacted with enthusiasm to his report. However, the hard core of the Peace Corps always looked a bit askance at the whole project. The UN volunteers idea was not particularly popular, since perhaps it would infringe on the Peace Corps' preeminence in that field. That was okay with me. The idea wasn't accepted with enthusiasm, but the die was cast, and it was obvious a UN Volunteer Corps would come into existence.

In less than two years, I had had the best of worlds and the worst of worlds. The experience caused me to really wonder about leaving the Foreign Service. I don't recall that anyone in the State Department ever said a positive word about the work I did for the Peace Corps, and when my tour ended in 1970 and I had to head back to the State Department, my life was not easy.

The establishment did not look favorably on my double desertion to the Peace Corps, and my last boss in Bogotá had given me a somewhat unfavorable personnel report due to my premature departure. I would have done much better from the Foreign Service point of view if I had swallowed my boredom and stuck with my language-training assignment. That seemed to make me something of a marked man. Thank heaven, I had gotten to know the head of the Canadian desk, who took a liking to me and offered me a job in his Washington office.

I grabbed it gratefully and went on to enjoy two years working on various Canadian matters, particularly the negotiations for the Great Lakes Water Quality Agreement. Complex environmental negotiations were involved, designed to clean up the lakes that were growing more and more polluted. Also, opportunities presented themselves for travel to such places as the Canadian Arctic and northern wilderness areas inhabited mostly by Canada's First Nations tribes. The discovery and exploitation of oil reserves in the north polar region made it a complex and fascinating area to cover. Sharing the region with the Soviets added to the tension. I became more and more reconciled to the fact that I was in the Foreign Service to stay.

My next assignment, in 1974, was a natural and successful progression, in Foreign Service terms. I was assigned to the political section of the embassy in Ottawa, and it got me somewhat into US politics. We were then deeply immersed in the Vietnam War, and Canada became a mecca for many fleeing the draft. We became the butt of much criticism about the war from Canadians, with the embassy at times the focal point. Our work often related very closely to what was going on in the US. I, in turn, became more and more interested in what was going on at home.

At this point, my father had retired from government service and accepted a number of nice jobs in the private sector, mostly involving his work on various Swiss boards of directors. My parents bought a house in Summit, New Jersey, and lived there until they became somewhat hobbled by age, and my mom by dementia. At that point they returned to Switzerland, where my father died in 1980 and my mother in 1981. A lot of people in Canada remembered them, and my father got a kick out of my Ottawa assignment.

It's funny how, after turning down an offer to work as a spy, I was occasionally asked if I worked as a CIA operative. I was even asked the question by the station chief in staid, old Ottawa, as we passed each other in the stairwell: "Hey, Ed, are you one of us?"

One reason may be because I was usually the one in an embassy most likely to take on assignments others didn't like, such as covering the Arctic regions. After one such trip, I even made the front page of the *Vancouver Sun*, Canada's leading West Coast paper. Some troublemaking Canadian who disliked the US went to the *Sun* and told them that he knew me and knew I worked for the CIA. What was the CIA doing snooping around the Canadian north and west? This was after the *Sun* ran a story on my trip.

My phone, and the embassy's, rang off their hooks. Ambassador William Porter, typically kind and solicitous, called me in, demanding to know the truth. For once, everything went my way. I asked them to look at the article and look again at the headline. The headline and story read something along the lines of "Ed Neff, US embassy employee, identified as CIA operative by Canadian coworker who knew him well at . . . ."

I pointed at it and said, "Anyone who claims to know me well knows I spell my name with one F." The embassy swung into action and demanded of the *Sun* that the informant spell my name. The *Sun* called me to verify the spelling, and I believe they even placed an innocent call to the perpetrator who matter-of-factly spelled my name with two Fs. I don't believe the paper apologized. A big anti-American balloon deflated with a big whoosh.

When my time in Ottawa came to a close, a good friend in the Foreign Service helped me with my next move. Larry Pezzullo and I had suffered together in Bogotá in the political section and he shared my deep misgivings about that post. Larry knew of my interest in US politics. Thanks to him, I applied for a State Department

Congressional fellowship for 1976–77. To my surprise, I won it. This sounded exciting and challenging, but—again—far removed from the usual Foreign Service assignment. Indeed, I would be working for Congress.

The first half of the year I spent with Senator Pete Dominici, a Republican representing New Mexico, whom I grew to admire. I was proud to work for and get to know him. After six months, I was supposed to move on to another job on the Hill, per the terms of the fellowship, and I decided to try the other party. I picked Rep. Max Baucus of Montana. I liked everything about him. He was young (close to my age) and a Democrat. What particularly pleased me was that he was a House member running for the Senate, so I would have some exposure to the heat of political competition.

The assignment could not have worked out better. I accompanied him on some of his campaign trips around Montana and worked with him to form positions on key issues in the contest. I was fortunate because I had spent four years working on the Canada desk, focused on US-Canadian environmental issues.

In fact, at this time a key topic in the Congress was negotiating the Great Lakes Water Quality Agreement. So I knew something about the issues. And, of course, Montana is a border state, so Canadian matters are important there. The issue was indeed important: how to counter increased deterioration in the shared lakes ringed by enormous industrial complexes spewing out great quantities of pollution. This affected a large segment of the American and Canadian populations, and negotiations brought us in touch with a huge variety of special interests.

I was a long-standing Democrat, but secretly I had to admit Republican Domenici was an easier person to work for. He had an excellent grasp of issues, since he had already served as a senator for a number of years, and he worked closely with staff. In defense of Max, he was newly elected to the Senate, one of its youngest and newest members, and he must have felt somewhat insecure about how to carry himself at the very beginning of his career (which ended gloriously a number of years later as chairman of the Senate Finance Committee).

It was beginning to dawn on me that I most enjoyed working *outside* the State Department. Much of the problem may have been a rebellious streak that made it difficult for me to conform to structure. Also, my expectations were obviously way off base. A Foreign Service officer was sent overseas to observe, report and comment on events. I, on the other hand, was happiest when able to immerse myself in surrounding events and be a part of the action.

It had taken me so long to realize it because I had often taken assignments that allowed me to play an active role (and were not on the usual career path): two assignments to the Peace Corps and work in the Congress—half my assignments! Those jobs obviously prolonged the decisive moment about my future. Stay, or take a huge step and abandon all I had done so far.

When my twelve months on the fellowship were up, and it was time to return to the State Department, I screwed up my courage and asked Max's administrative assistant, Steve Browning, if Max might be looking for staff as he opened his new office in the Senate. Especially thanks to my friendship with Steve—a truly great guy serving his country in the Congress—Max offered me the job of legislative director in his office, a top job.

I accepted with alacrity. With immense relief, I tendered my resignation from the Foreign Service. Thus ended eighteen years of off-and-on-again work for the State Department and my career as a Foreign Service officer. I was so glad to be finished with its rigid structures and weird priorities. I was tired of the bureaucracy, the lack of creative challenge, the need to keep the boss happy even when he was an enormous disappointment.

In hindsight, I wish I hadn't been so stuck on the Foreign Service. After I made that career choice my freshman year, I just never thought about it again. The Foreign Service was for me. No matter how unhappy I might have been at times, it never occurred to me

Senator Max Baucus and me around 1978.

that I should just quit and look elsewhere. Maybe this was because of an unconscious unwillingness to admit defeat.

Looking back, I realize how many of my travails were of my own making. I was unwilling to accept a personnel structure that did not encourage freelancing but expected great respect for rank and privilege. Its people tended to be more scholarly and analytical, whereas I was more of an activist. I wanted to go out on my own, explore people and events. But I was usually fond of many people I worked with.

I think my biggest problem, which I didn't recognize until years later, was that the career objective of a Foreign Service officer—to head a diplomatic mission—no longer appealed to me. The thought of spending many years working at what I often found boring to finally achieve (if I was enormously fortunate) my goal a few years before retirement was not of interest to me. There were lots of better ways to spend what was left of my life.

My dad, though disconcerted about my departure from my foreign service career, supported me morally and philosophically as best he could. It took time for him, but I think he eventually gave me some grudging respect for the new job in the Senate. It helped when he noted the life I began to lead, flying around the country in private jets, mingling with top political leaders one reads about in the papers, and attending all sorts of national and international events.

But still, it must have been disappointing for him. I am sure he was proud I had followed in his footsteps, but now I had left the diplomatic world. What he probably worried about the most was the loss of the security a government job gave me. For his generation, security was of paramount importance. He even managed to get me a lucrative job offer with a Swiss Bank (I felt very guilty when I turned it down, but my dad shrugged). I knew for certain that he would always be there for me and ready to help as best he could.

Legislative director for Senator Baucus sounded like an awesome job, but under Max's management structure, the real chief was his administrative assistant, Steve Browning. I filled in where there were gaps in Max's staff, but I honestly felt rather lost at times, and Steve would come to the rescue. I must admit in hindsight that Max was very patient with me.

Politics were also incredibly insecure. One never knew when one's boss might suddenly change committees or even lose an election. On several occasions I was close to being ousted, because I was out of my depth on some subjects handled in the Senate. Life there revolved around the legislative process, about which I was not experienced. I'm sure there were times when Max wondered about me and what I was contributing to his office. I was valuable to him when he was involved in the political process, because I understood and enjoyed that, but elections came up just every two years.

When the focus turned to political issues, it was so challenging to work on issues of national importance, propose solutions to be followed, hear strongly expressed opposing views, seek compromises, and so on. These challenges were ultimately decided by the senator, but still it was exciting to hear the debates, express one's view as a loyal staffer, and then observe the ultimate denouement in legislative action. With time, I became more self-confident as I learned how things worked, and as I developed good contacts in the organization.

Much of the time was spent worrying about legislation, amendments to laws, government regulations, the hearing process, and so on. It was fascinating, and one really had to know the law and the process well to succeed. I did my best and will forever consider it a tremendous learning experience.

The power of Congress was always evident, even at the simplest level. At the State Department, we were regularly the recipient of some congressional inquiry, usually prompted by an unhappy constituent demanding immediate action. Usually these were personal in nature, but members of Congress always felt obliged to handle such things on a priority basis. So there was no hesitation to give the State Department a hard time if it did not respond rapidly enough.

It was also disconcerting to realize how many really important issues the senator would have to vote on after the briefest review and consideration (hence the importance of good staff work). There were some issues that received time and study, and these were usually matters pertinent to the committee on which he served. But all bills, no matter what, were always important to someone.

Again, my personality intruded, and as time passed I was became unhappy and disgruntled with the Senate job, glamorous as it seemed. In fact, seeing politics from the inside could be as disillusioning as working for the State Department. Baucus himself was a nice enough person but unpredictable and disinterested when it came to office administration. Steve Browning handled all that.

All Baucus's actions seemed motivated by the politics of the moment, and it was often hard to discern what path he was taking. It was truly helter-skelter. In fairness, all this was new to Baucus, too. He obviously grew a lot in the job, ultimately becoming chairman of the Finance Committee and doing a good job. He was a decent person; I have always liked him.

When I signed on with Baucus, I told him I hoped to stay for five years. After that, I would be eligible for retirement under Senate rules and would move on. One's employment in the office of a member of Congress was based on the representative's whim and not on a written contract. But I made it through my term, and after five years I left. No tears were shed on either side. I was very happy and a bit nervous as I faced an uncertain future.

That was it. I never dreamed it would end so favorably. Happening across that ad for a language school in the "Businesses for Sale" section changed my life. My business gave me enormous satisfaction and the freedom to follow my passions.

Opening schools abroad aroused my entrepreneurial spirit to pursue a more creative—and in many ways even more daunting— adventure. In the third chapter of my professional life, I became a film producer.

chapter seven

Entering the
Film Industry

Opening and managing for-profit language schools wherever such
an endeavor was well-received continued successfully through the
early 2000s. Schools in Japan and Mongolia had provided fascinating experiences that whetted my appetite for more such ventures. I
became bolder, and when an opportunity presented itself to open
a school in Hanoi, capital of the nation we had fought so bitterly
and so tragically, it seemed the right time to investigate with an
open and positive mind.

My warm reception in Hanoi really touched me. I was so impressed by the Vietnamese character—a people who throughout
history have been exploited and have suffered. The Vietnam War,
the worst and longest war our country had ever fought, was history.
After quite a few years of continued conflict (the next one against
the Chinese) and near disaster in post-war economic management,
the Vietnamese finally accepted the fact that friendship with the US
might be beneficial. Maybe Western economic theories were not
all bad. In fact, fairly quickly, Vietnam went from near economic
collapse to being one of the strongest economies in Southeast Asia.

On the American side, we had long outgrown ardent anti-communism and appeared ready for rapprochement. Many former combat veterans in the US made their voices heard: We had an obligation to help the Vietnamese in their struggles for survival.

As I got to know Vietnam, my restless spirit took over. I was fascinated by the opportunities there. The foremost of these was a curious itch I had to take more seriously a hobby I had pursued from a very young age—photography. As a young boy, I remember my father sharing his interest in photography, developing and printing his own pictures.

It happened the first summer after World War II ended, and it became at least modestly feasible to travel to war-torn Europe again. My father had to report to his supervisors in Bern what was happening in the US as reconstruction in Europe was underway. He had already gone once almost as soon as the war ended, but now that peace had prevailed for a brief while, he wanted all of us to meet the family again.

As soon as summer vacation started, he bundled us all into a TWA DC-4 (the only commercial transportation available that soon after the war), and we embarked on a four-day plane trip from New York City to Zurich. My goodness, was that exciting for a twelve-year-old! I probably annoyed many of the other passengers, because I didn't get airsick, never have. Despite the substantial turbulence, I wandered up and down the aisle when I wasn't eating or sleeping.

It took four days because the plane could not fly at today's altitudes; it had to lumber through altitudes of 5–6,000 feet or wait at the airport for disturbances to pass. The result was an overnight stop in Gander, Newfoundland, after eight hours because of bad weather over the Atlantic. Then, a *very* bumpy ten hours to Shannon, Ireland, where we stopped for breakfast. In a few more hours we reached Paris for lunch (still lining the runways were destroyed airplanes from the war). And, finally, Zurich.

There we were in Switzerland, visiting all the relatives and staying with my grandmother. My father had been raised partially in that house, and as a young boy he had gotten interested in photography.

He had set up a small, very primitive darkroom, where he learned to develop his films. Now, some fifty years later, he was teaching me how to do the same thing in his ancient darkroom, much to my enjoyment. For the rest of my life, photography interested me.

As a student at Phillips Academy, Andover, I had joined the photography club. As an enlisted man in the Army, I made full use of the well-equipped labs available to military people to pursue their interests. Through the subsequent years, I always took cameras with me everywhere and enjoyed all the pleasures of the hobby. Eventually, that hobby evolved into an interest in film, precipitated by my wonderful experience in Vietnam.

I was so amazed, even overwhelmed, by the positive attitude of the Vietnamese people as Americans began to trickle back into the country, that I had a great desire to produce a film on how the two countries reconciled to form a solid new friendship. Never mind that I had never produced a film of any sort and had not even the most rudimentary knowledge of film production.

It wasn't the first time I had run headlong into a new endeavor for which I was unqualified. What had I known about running a language school? Nothing. But I spoke several languages, and that challenge didn't terrify me at all. I hired good staff, and the rest I learned on the job.

My dad would have had a bird had he lived long enough to witness these peregrinations. He thought one had to be serious, dedicate oneself to one's career, excel in it, and retire with honors, as he had. His career as a Swiss government official was indeed remarkable, and I wish I could have been as successful. Here I was, flitting from one perch to another and loving it.

I was stupid and naïve as I entered the film industry. The fact that, despite all odds, we ended up producing a pretty good flick attests to the fact that the good Lord watches over his less-gifted.

I talked to my language-school partner, Thuy Thu Do, in Hanoi to see what she thought. She approved, with a little bit of hesitation, but not enough to deter her. A few others, including some members of her family, were not so sure. They saw risks in the subject, possible opposition from the government, and popular rejection of the theme. But with my partner's support, I decided to go ahead.

Filled with optimism, I started Santis Productions, LLC, a small film production company incorporated in Arlington in 2006. It was natural that my film production creation also be considered a part of Santis, the umbrella corporation for my language schools.

I found in my school in Washington talented teachers whose first love was film production. They gladly joined me in this new undertaking, well aware that I could not pay them much. It would be a work of love. One such teacher was a very bright young Colombian American, Mabel Cristina, who taught Spanish in my school and had majored in film production in college. She brought with her a bright young Korean American, Damon Chung, who worked as an IT specialist but much preferred the creative world of film production.

We were all excited and gearing up for our first trip to Vietnam to start filming when the worst happened: Mabel became very ill. I had to find a substitute very quickly; we were leaving in about two weeks.

Fortunately, as we worked our way toward Vietnam, I became acquainted with some very good souls who knew something about the industry in Vietnam. The first introduction was to an independent film producer who offered to help. Unfortunately, he gave us a nice but inexperienced young cinematographer whom we had to let go.

Other acquaintances stepped in and made a point of introducing us to people at the Vietnamese national television network. One thing led to another until I was introduced to their front line cinematographers, Nguyen Manh Cuong and Nguyen Viet Hoang, who were willing to take responsibility. The one thing I really knew was that with my total lack of experience and knowledge, I needed to find real pros. These men never disappointed me.

Before we started filming, I wanted to find some genuine US combat vets who had lived and survived the experience. Then I needed some Vietnamese citizens to act as facilitators and interpreters. I did not have to look further than the people who were now working for my school, including my business partner, who brought along some of her family (not surprisingly!). They all ended up contributing enormously to the success of the film.

We traveled to and filmed many of the major battlefields, the underground tunnels of the Vietcong, the prisons, the burial grounds, and the memorials. We included the saints on both sides who sought to repatriate the remains of those who died there, and the people who created Friendship Village to help those who suffered from the American use of Agent Orange. We even filmed private American groups and individuals who were returning to Vietnam to see how they might help reconstruction.

This was one of the most memorable journeys I ever took in my lifetime. To this day I remain friends with several of the vets, including Gary Cunningham, a former helicopter pilot who flew some 800 missions, and Chip Troiano, who fought in some of the most dangerous and fearful battles of the war.

I will remain forever indebted to those who threw in their lots with me. After we completed filming, a recovered Mabel and Damon worked together on all the technical editing. It took more than two years to complete the film. Unfortunately, we were never able to reconnect long-term with Mabel, who went off to her own successful career.

To this day, one of the most important people in my professional film production life is Damon Chung, who continued for a long time to make our subsequent films unforgettable through his artful IT skills. I don't know what I would have done without him.

Much to my surprise, the film ended up being quite a success. The Vietnamese reacted overwhelmingly favorably, and their national television network broadcast it multiple times on primetime on the occasion of their national day. They even broadcast it worldwide on their international network. Reactions in the US were equally enthusiastic, as it was shown in many educational and film centers. The US military HULU TV channel asked if they could air it.

One of the most thrilling outcomes was that suddenly my partner, Thuy, who not only had encouraged me but also taken a part in the production, was a celebrity! She starred in several segments of the film. She and our school achieved fame. The city government was so pleased they gave our school very large exclusive contracts to teach English in the city elementary schools, which of course were to Thuy's benefit.

I never dreamed it would be so well received—my first film with no prior experience in the industry. My effort ended more successfully than expected, and that energized me. Why not try another film? I had no bright ideas, but dumb fate came to my rescue again.

A segment of the Vietnam film showed how Americans were investing in Vietnam in the post-war era. A significant investor was a casual friend, Ed Story, whom I had met in Mongolia. A Texas oil man, Ed had worked the limited oil fields there. Now he was turning to the oil-rich fields in the South China Sea. I met him in Vietnam, and he helicoptered us out to the oil rig somewhere in the middle of the sea. That was pretty exciting. We had a very good interview about US investments in Vietnam.

Like so many others, Ed asked what our next film would be. When I told him I didn't know yet, he suggested doing a film about elephant polo.

Elephant polo? What on earth was that? It turned out it was quite a popular sport in Thailand and elsewhere in that part of the world, wherever there were elephants. It is played just like regular polo, except the steeds are elephants. Ed was enamored with the sport and competed regularly in tournaments. In fact, he was soon going to compete in the king's tournament in northern Thailand. Why didn't I film the event?

As you can imagine, it took me about a millisecond to agree.

The tournament was to take place near Chiang Rai, in the far northern corner of Thailand, near where the Mekong River forms the border with Laos and Burma. The area had always been a hotbed of extremism and was still mostly underdeveloped, with thick jungles and dangerous wildlife. For a long time the area was known as the golden triangle of drug running and drug production. After the drug trade died down, a large opium museum opened there, showing how the industry developed and dominated the area for years—a truly fascinating place to visit.

Soon I was on my way to Thailand with cinematographer Dennis Kane, a nice person who was highly qualified as one of the *National Geographic*'s former lead photographers. He had recently retired and was looking for some freelance work. We soon found ourselves ensconced in a gorgeous, five-star hotel in the middle of the jungle not far from Chiang Rai.

It fascinated me to learn that although the drug trade had been greatly reduced, remnants of it still existed. I casually mentioned to one of the hotel administrators that it would be fascinating to meet and interview the current head of the local drug cartel such as it was, and I wondered if such a person existed.

The man asked if I were serious. I said sure, but I would not do anything illegal or dangerous. He told me he would check, and someone would get in touch with me. I started to get nervous and hoped no one would come. Alas, the next day a man quietly sidled up to me in the restaurant and introduced himself as someone who could arrange such an interview, but there would be conditions.

First, bring $10,000 in cash. Second, come alone, unarmed. Third, be prepared for a three-day journey on horseback into the deep jungle to reach the hidden camp. I could never meet those conditions. I wasn't crazy. The man looked disappointed, but said okay, and then he melted into the surrounding crowd of hotel guests. I never saw him again.

I went back to filming the elephant polo tournament. That indeed was fascinating to watch and be a part of. I learned so much about the elephant culture and the people's love for these huge beasts. Gentle and intelligent, elephants performed remarkable feats in service to the people who bonded with them. Research has found that elephants do create bonds with humans, and there was a successful program bringing elephants and autistic children together as therapy. The king's cup tournament was partially a fundraiser for this activity.

The world of elephants was intriguing, but my filmmaking talents and contacts were not broad enough to expand on that topic beyond filming the tournament. There are so many topics to cover, like the elephants used by their *mahouts* (owners) to beg for donations by roaming the city streets and seeking tourists and others who might give them money. But I couldn't figure out a way to film that.

It was great fun to wander among the elephants, feed and caress them, and speak to their *mahouts*, if only briefly. Our film was pretty good, if I do say so myself, but not particularly successful. The subject was too narrow, and we lacked good PR and a vehicle to help spread the word. Still, I never regretted the undertaking, nor the people and culture I encountered. It was a wonderful experience.

I am eternally grateful to Ed Story for inspiring this film and helping so much in its production. Those wonderful beasts owe Ed a debt of gratitude as well. To this day, he is still dedicated to elephant preservation; he founded a non-profit organization, The Elephant Story, for elephant protection. Ed remains a good personal friend.

I then had two films under my belt, one very successful, the second successful in a more limited way. They might have done even better had I not felt unequal to the challenge of promoting my films publicly and commercially.

I knew how hard it was to break into the film industry for profit. Early on, I decided to make films for the sheer challenge and enjoyment of doing so, hoping that by putting it out there, people would learn something they had not known before. That was my guiding principle all through my filming career.

We ended up with some commercial successes when a promoter would see the film and ask to distribute it. But, generally, our films were distributed through educational or other private channels, and positive feedback would often filter back to us. That was satisfaction enough.

Since profit was not a motive, part of the fun was pulling together teams who shared my enthusiasm and were happy to work, as long as I covered incidental and travel expenses, which I was glad to do. Many of these were young people eager for the challenge and the learning experience. I hasten to add that many of these younger folk were immensely talented. I always thanked my lucky stars they came to me, not with dollar signs in their eyes, but motivated by adventure and eagerness to try new things.

Of course, I had to hire at the proper moments first-line talent in technical fields, like cinematography, if I wanted to be successful. These were usually old and trusted friends like Damon Chung and Richard Needham.

As time passed, I found the single most costly item was usually the camera. You had to have good cameras and good lenses, and we usually ended up renting them. Even that could cost thousands of dollars for a week or two. The cost of camera rental easily reached $30,000 to $40,000; it would cost much more to buy one.

The film team usually included a translator/interpreter and script developer. Actually, most of the time I took the lead there. This was usually not so hard; rarely did we have memorized scripts, and interviews were also unrehearsed. Since we always tried to film people in their natural habitat, we never had fashion consultants, set designers, or anything like that.

Once the field team shot the film, a completely different operation took over—the technical perfectionists. Here we used professional laboratories that had all the technical equipment to fine tune, edit, color-code, modify, improve, and cut. Again, not cheap, but essential.

One aspect of the process was our desire to produce films in several languages. Our Mongolian films have both English and Mongolian soundtracks, and others have French subtitles or soundtracks. This was an added expense, but one I really thought essential. I suppose this should not be surprising, given my background!

After our elephant film, I went back to the land I loved—Mongolia. Elections were coming up that were going to be crucial to that land's future. The world had discovered the enormous mineral wealth of that country, catapulting it from one of the poorest countries in the world to potentially one of the richest. Gold, copper, iron, silver, rare earth minerals, you name it, Mongolia had it in abundance.

At its doorstep was China, a nation exploding with growth and an intense desire for development that required huge amounts of coal, copper, and other minerals. Soon the world's richest coal mine was in operation fifty miles from the Chinese border in the middle of Mongolia's Gobi Desert.

My most loyal film crew, from left to right: Damon
Chung, his wife MK, Meiyue (May) Zhou, and me.

This prompted mixed emotions. On the one hand, one could rejoice that poverty might diminish, standards of living rise, and general well-being improve. On the flip side, one could also see massive deterioration in the environment, destruction of ancient and highly respected traditions, and the beauty of the land slowly being sacrificed. Also, a nomadic culture could be grievously challenged and possibly even destroyed.

I thought a film about these conflicting emotions just might cause people to reflect before embarking on new and untested mining ventures.

A society that has survived generations of great poverty, where the simple act of human survival often depended on friend or family to support and help, cannot easily escape the culture of interdependence. When a family member suddenly had a good job or was successful in some endeavor, it was not surprising that the individual would want to help his or her family members survive. The result was a job going to a family member rather than to an outsider.

We may call it nepotism or bias in the West. To Mongolians, it was only natural. But it led to destructive outcomes, where unemployed family members lost initiative and had no problem living off the work of the successful. The culture often failed to breed ambition. The unchallenged expectation was that the successful one had to help, no matter what.

One of the first stories that caught my attention was that of a poor rural nomad, one of the Tsaatan (reindeer tribe), who had gotten swept up in the mining frenzy. The humble folk of the Tsaatan had learned that the creeks and shores of the rivers they forded daily were laden with gold. All it took was a pan for panning. Indeed, at least some of those who tried soon found gold and made more money than they had ever dreamed of. The stampede started.

So some of my friends among the nomadic reindeer herders used their spare time to pan for gold as they crossed those rivers and streams. Some would load up their gear and go out to places found to be particularly fertile. Very quickly these sites became large outlaw communities. It was illegal to mine for gold without a permit, but they did so anyway. Inevitably these became rather dangerous places, as hundreds might come together in search of gold.

The husband of one of the families I knew did that. In anticipation of newfound wealth, he had sent his family to Ulaan Bataar to start a more prosperous life. Meanwhile, he had packed up and ridden his horse to the nearest gold-seeking community. It was at this point that I met his family. His wife was struggling to find a job, and his children were living a hard life.

She told me stoically that indeed her husband had struck it rich. Unfortunately, he told one of his acquaintances at the camp of his success and of his intention to return to the big city.

He left the camp and was never seen again alive. Apparently, thieves set upon him as he followed the trail out of the mountains, killed him, and dumped his body in a shallow pond. All his gold and belongings were stolen. Nothing was recovered. His only mistake was talking too much.

His widow told me the story in brief sentences with eyes downcast. She was now the family breadwinner, but with no real job. She had been a teacher and hoped some day to find such a job in the big city, but it would take time. Meanwhile, she took any job she could find, from street sweeper to housemaid.

I had gotten to know this family on one of my trips up into the hinterland, the high steppes, wherever the nomads lived (and where I loved to visit). We had become friends of sorts, and we'd spend evenings in their tent chatting (through family interpreters). We sat and ate the same food they ate, humble and plain, and offered to me without hesitancy or expectation. Fermented mare's milk was the usual beverage.

Their annual income was probably not more than $200–$300 a year, if that. They truly lived off the land 365 days a year, in the relative warmth of summer to the truly frigid winter (−30 to −40 degrees Fahrenheit).

It was particularly sad that all the family's plans and hopes centered around the aspirations of one of their daughters, around ten or eleven years old. They had discovered as she grew up on the steppes that she was athletically gifted; she had grown quite proficient in contortionism. She could twist her young body any which way, and the family hoped her abilities would carry her to circus stardom. The decision to move to Ulaan Bataar was predicated on the thought that she would perfect her skills in Mongolia's famed circus school. Her father's money from gold mining would be spent fostering her ambition.

Now all those hopes lay in ruins. Even then, from the pittance she earned, the mother put aside a few pennies to pay for training for her daughter. When I heard of their tragic turn of fortune, a thought occurred.

One of my Mongolian friends, Gunkukyag Natsag ("Ganna"), is a gifted impresario whose dream is to build Buddhist peace pagodas all over East Asia. He produced Mongolian shows that toured around

Asia. Thanks to a chance encounter with a French promoter, Ganna was invited to bring his troupe to France and eventually elsewhere, and he began to get a name for himself and his troupe (many were family members!).

I thought it would be neat to bring Ganna to Washington, DC. He had Mongolian dancers, throat singers and performers. What more could clinch it? How about a young Mongolian girl contortionist? Mongolians are known in the circus world for their skills in contortion. If he would take her on, we would try to get the group to perform at the Kennedy Center and at Arlington's Artisphere Theater. This of course thrilled Ganna, and very quickly the girl became part of his program.

It took a couple of months to set it all up, and many Mongolians leapt in to help the girl. One lady in the show, Chimgee Haltarhuu, had been a circus performer herself and had her own show in Minnesota. She offered to help, as did others, to watch over the young girl alone in the US. We of course would take care of her and another young Mongolian singer, who made a nice pair of female performers, while they were in Washington.

The Kennedy Center ended up being enthusiastic and most helpful in getting our show on their stage. I think they were touched by our story. It was a huge success, with a standing-room-only audience.

By the time they got back to Mongolia, they had achieved some fame and our contortionist was given a scholarship at the circus school. Today she is a steady show-business employee, I believe.

Looking back, I enjoyed making the film about Mongolian mining, *Mongolia—Mining Challenges a Civilization*, and interviewing the hardworking and, frankly, exploited workers who labored deep in the mines. Mining is hard and risky work – and there was always the incentive to work as an independent (and illegal) "ninja" worker, as they called themselves. Publicizing their hardships certainly could do no harm. Many would descend on a mine pit recently dug by the mining company and start sifting through the discarded piles of dirt. Gold could always to be found, obviously in much reduced quantity, but it was hard work and not profitable enough for the companies to do the same. So they winked at the individual efforts, and the ninjas would dig deep holes with primitive tools, often going twenty-five to fifty feet into the earth piled around the pits.

Lacking proper support to shore up the walls, these holes would occasionally collapse on the toiling workers, causing injuries and even death. But the ninjas toiled on. They were able to make relatively good money without paying taxes or other costs. Of course, if the ninjas found one pile particularly rich, the company would oust them and move back in.

We also interviewed the truck drivers who drove the twenty-two-wheel giants that carried the output of huge coal mines in the Gobi fifty miles south to the Chinese border. The Chinese made them dump their loads at the border; they did not want them to profit from trucking inside China. By international agreement, the truckers were supposed to be ninety percent Mongolians. But the Chinese just used their own truckers, causing great resentment among Mongolians.

In addition, completely ignoring the law, many Chinese companies crossed the border illegally and opened their own mines using their labor and trucks. It was not a happy situation. We would travel the Gobi Desert and pass a huge mining operation and be told the whole thing was an illegal Chinese mine operating with impunity. Mongolia did little to enforce the law.

The film we produced ended up being very well received by most, excluding the mining company people. It went on to win prizes at the Vermont International Film Festival and the New England Film Festival. It was shown widely in Mongolia as elections approached. Not surprisingly, mining and its effects were a major theme of the election. I can't help but think our film had some impact on the electorate.

I was told even the president of Mongolia saw it and indicated enthusiasm for its conclusions. The mining companies were obviously not happy. One erstwhile filmmaker colleague even warned me to watch my back; people often played rough out in the back country. Thankfully, nothing ever happened, not even threats. Mongolia evidently had progressed from earlier days when possibly more aggressive Soviet protocols were followed.

The elections were praised by impartial observers as being relatively free and open. Mongolia remains one of the few "new" countries of the world with a succession of free and open elections with peaceful transfers of power. While many things played into producing such an outcome, I like to think our film had a small role in encouraging peaceful debate.

One of the happy surprises of this film was reconnecting with a Harvard classmate of mine, Doug Hartley. He had lived in my dorm freshman year and had graduated from Eton, in England. He was friendly, very musical, and had a bit of a British accent although he was half-American.

I'll never forget teasing him, "Hey, Doug! You're such a good musician, play Tchaikovsky's piano concerto for me!" Doug pushed back from the piano, looked thoughtfully at me, hummed to himself a moment, and then suddenly swooped down on the keyboard and BANG, CRASH! Out poured the requested opus, all played by ear. I kept quiet after that.

Doug had also joined the US Foreign Service after graduation and eventually returned to the DC area, where we renewed our friendship. Meeting Doug again reminded me of his enormous musical talent, and I wondered if he might be interested in composing a musical score to accompany the Mongolian mining film. He was enthusiastic about the idea, and there began a partnership that lasted through the years. He has composed musical background for almost all the films we produced.

After the Mongolian mining documentary, we made several shorter films more or less for the fun of it. One was on Mongolian bagel-baking. We did another one for *The Washington Post* on Mongolian mask-making.

Chronologically, our next film dealt with the disappearance of remote languages and cultures. My continuing interest in Mongolia made me want to report on the slow death of the Tuvan language, most of whose speakers were members of the Tsaatan tribe of reindeer herders. Only some fifty families still clung to their Tuvan roots, and they were trying very hard to preserve what they had. The whole thing saddened me greatly.

Most unfortunately, as I concluded an interview with an excellent observer of the Mongolian scene, I stood up and then proceeded to collapse into the furniture. I had suffered a minor stroke. Others had to finish the filming, and after a few days in the hospital, I was headed for home.

I had to rely on friends and surrogates to do the work on this film. I am very proud of how everyone came unselfishly to help, and we ended by producing a credible story about struggles to keep ancient cultures and languages alive despite the pressures of modernization.

In all my interactions with the Tsaatan, my own life became so enriched by learning of their day-to-day hardy survival, living as family groups and sharing hardships among each other. There were frequent experiences that will forever remain close to my heart and never be forgotten.

For no particular reason, I was drawn to the Lake Hovsgol area, near the Russian border and not too far from Lake Baikal. It is the largest lake in Mongolia, a beautiful environment with mountains, wilderness, and exotic scenery. Near there were the Tsaatan.

I had been told by Mongolians in Ulaan Baatar who were trying to help the Tsaatan that the year before had been disastrous for them. A winter *Zud*, or calamitous freeze, had killed many of their horses, their only means of transportation. Lacking horses, they were forced to use their reindeer for transportation. While the reindeer could do it for short distances, they were not strong enough to become permanent beasts of burden.

When I first met the Tsaatan in their environment, I was enormously impressed and fascinated. I had gone up there previously just to visit; the lake shore had a few sites for camping and rough tourism. But after the *Zud*, everything was falling apart.

I learned that for about $1,000 we could buy twenty horses, and the Tsaatan could each have a new horse. It was an easy decision to make. The next spring when I went up to Lake Hovsgol, we stopped in the valley and, with some astute bargaining, purchased the horses. Two days later, we drove the herd up into the mountains so that I could gift them to the Tsaatan.

There was a ceremony with a blessing of the horses with mare's milk. It was very quiet and solemn. In their culture they all help each other, from youngest to oldest, and never rely on outsiders. In fact, they are so unaccustomed to being offered or accepting gifts, I don't believe there is a word in the Mongolian language that corresponds to our "thank you." But I could feel their happiness and gratitude.

Afterward, every now and then a man sidled up to me as I sat on my horse and thrust something into my hand. I'd look down and there might be a hand-carved object made from reindeer horn. Or a woman would approach shyly and give me as a souvenir, some small item she may have woven. When we left their encampment to return to our world, they were all there, standing silently and bidding farewell.

Several years later, one told me that the whole community looked upon that moment as a transcendental point in their lives. They turned from seeing only a bleak life filled with increased hardship to a life of renewed hope. This meshed with their Buddhist beliefs. All for the few dollars spent on some horses. What an enormous reward that was for me.

My film crew colleagues and I formed many friendships with the wonderful Mongolian families we met, and we tried to stay in touch. On one occasion, we planned a return visit to continue the friendship and to see if there was any way we could help them while we filmed in the surrounding area. Shortly before our arrival, we heard the tragic news of a family murder. We immediately thought we should cancel our trip, but the locals insisted we come on.

This sad tale occurred in the family of one of my closest friends in Mongolia's nomadic society. They had always shown me great kindness and patience whenever I visited their most remote home territory, far from civilization, near the Siberian border. When we arrived, we found that Batzaya, the father, had been evacuated to Ulaan Baatar for treatment of near-fatal knife wounds.

A couple of weeks earlier, the family had been awakened in the middle of the night by loud and violent screams coming from the tent next to theirs, a tent occupied by their adopted son and his seventeen-year-old bride. Batzaya leapt up and rushed over.

He burst into the tent just in time to see his son, face contorted, standing over his wife and thrusting his knife into her body as she screamed and twisted in pain. Again and again he struck, stopping only when Batzaya tackled him and tried to seize the knife. The son turned and, in a maniacal rage, thrust the knife into Batzaya.

Now others rushed in to help. The son was overwhelmed and dropped the knife. He fled the tent and ran into the darkness of the surrounding woods. All attention turned to Batzaya and the girl. It was immediately apparent that the girl was dying if not already dead. Batzaya was bleeding profusely from wounds to his arms and shoulders. Primitive first aid was administered.

By now dawn was coming and the people began to look around for the son. They had camped in a small clearing of the dense forest, so the only place for the son to go was deeper in the forest.

The community members took off searching in different directions. It did not take long before one of the son's sisters let out a horrible shriek. She had found him. He was dead, hanging from a tree limb, having chosen to commit suicide.

Batzaya was cared for as best as possible in the camp. In testimony to the incredible toughness of these remote nomads, as soon as he could be put on a horse, they took him to the nearest Jeep to transport him to the closest rural health clinic—six hours away. Again, when he was deemed strong enough for travel, he was loaded onto a bus and transported twelve hours to Ulaan Baatar and relatively modern health facilities. They kept him there over a month before he was allowed to return home. His arm and shoulder were permanently damaged, but not seriously enough to disable him.

Eventually, a policeman came to their site to investigate what happened and file a report with the distant police force. Funerals are simple and not particularly ceremonial. The deceased is simply transported to a nearby mountain designated as holy, and the remains are carried up the slope and deposited on the ground. The body is eventually consumed by wild animals or just simply decays. No one ever returns to the site. For them, the human soul is immortal, and death is nothing other than the beginning of a new life.

My film production company next ventured to Africa to document a Senegalese success story. One day in a conversation with a friend who knew Senegal, we reminisced about days we had spent there. Senegal had been my first foreign service assignment, from 1960 to 1962, the most critical moment in Senegalese history. Charles de Gaulle had just passed through and said all former French colonies should be given their independence – a historic occasion.

As we talked about such events, I wondered out loud how lucky Senegal was that it had not been taken over by radical Islam. There were radical Islamic fundamentalists in the north, in Libya and elsewhere, and the wild Boco Haram in Nigeria. Yet Senegal remained peaceful and quiet, its population content and working industriously for their own future. I wondered why.

The reply from the Senegalese people I spoke with was immediate: It was because of the women of Senegal. The mothers just flatly refused to allow their sons to go off to join radical Islamists, and they rejected efforts to teach violence to their young people. It was also much in their favor that the brand of Islam practiced in Senegal was one of great peace and nonconfrontation. Their Islamic religion taught brotherhood and love.

What an idea that was—to produce a film about the women of Senegal and their influence on the course of that nation. It didn't take long to pull together a group of interested individuals to form a filming team. We had the help of some very intelligent and knowledgeable Senegalese, including a former TV broadcaster and a woman who had worked for me as a French teacher in my school in Washington. Andrea Sachs from *The Washington Post* joined us as well.

It was great fun and so wonderful to revisit a place where I had spent the first two years of my foreign service career. How things had changed, yet how many things remained the same! We traveled around the country, visiting rural and urban sites, interviewing a wide cross-section of the population. We learned that not everything had been easy in Senegal's past, especially for the women, solidifying my admiration for them and for their accomplishments. So many things had been stacked against them, yet with patience, great wisdom, and relatively little strife, they achieved their objectives.

Two aspects of their society were particularly difficult for them to overcome, both stemming from traditional practices going back centuries. The first was the practice of marrying child brides. For centuries, little girls as young as nine or ten would be given away in marriage. By the time they were twelve or thirteen, the chances were good that they would have been impregnated and died. It was the women of Senegal, aided by sympathetic men and Islamic leaders, who fought against this barbaric custom. Strict laws were passed forbidding marriage prior to age eighteen. Today, child brides are found only in the most rural and underdeveloped parts of the country.

The other extremely detrimental practice was that of female circumcision, an ancient tradition used to assure the fidelity of a man's wife. This practice existed for hundreds and hundreds of years, if not longer. A very painful and dangerous surgery, it resulted in many deaths and disfigurements. Finally, the women rebelled, again joined by many sympathetic men and religious leaders. It was a slow process, with opposition coming from many circles. Paradoxically, much resistance came from the young girls themselves, who feared that if they did not undergo the surgery they would never be married. What man, they wondered, would want to marry a woman who might lust after another man?

Wisdom and patience eventually prevailed. Today, like child brides, one finds this practice only in the most remote and isolated places. Female circumcision has virtually been eliminated in Senegal. By comparison, in the neighboring nation of Mali, still heavily influenced by fundamental Islamists, eighty to ninety percent of girls suffer this procedure.

Ours was the first film about Senegal in a long time. The Senegalese ambassador in Washington insisted on premiering it at his embassy, and it simultaneously premiered at the US embassy in

Dakar. It was picked up by the commercial distributor SnagFilms.

After completing the Senegalese film, the next venture was a fun film recording the 65th reunion of my class at Andover. It was a joy to go back to the school.

Age and a lack of inspiration led to a decline in my film production activities, but I did undertake an ambitious effort to film the Dalai Lama. My friend Ganna, the impresario, was working on the first of his many planned Buddhist Peace Pagodas in Mongolia, and he wanted to obtain the Dalai Lama's approval for this endeavor. Was I interested in filming such a meeting in December 2014? It meant travelling to the Dalai Lama's home in Dharamshala, India.

I signed on. Not too long after, my faithful crew and I were on the plane to India. We landed in Delhi, then drove to Dharamshala to await filming. Dharamshala, in the foothills of the Himalayas, is a fascinating and beautiful place. Surrounded by high hills and lush forests, the city was filled with monks and hordes of other people. Monkeys, cows, and other animals wandered the streets.

When we appeared at the front door to the Dalai Lama's center, we were ushered into a waiting room. There were armed guards all over the place. One of the guards stopped us. "No cameras," he said. What did they mean, "no cameras?" That was our purpose for being there. They forbade our entry. Totally crestfallen, we fell back and watched others file in. What had happened?

Those who were supposed to arrange our visit had neglected to tell the center we would have cameras. In their defense, they were probably as surprised as we that we were forbidden to bring cameras. We were clearly identified as filmmakers. No one had known or imagined the very tight security around the Dalai Lama. To get approval, if given, would undoubtedly have taken weeks of paperwork.

So the whole purpose for our trip fell through. The Dalai's staff was apologetic and hoped we understood. They invited us into several other meetings with His Holiness, including a private one with him and Ganna, where the Dalai Lama chatted comfortably with us.

The Dalai Lama himself turned out to be a delightful, gentle person with a charismatic yet humble bearing, easy to talk to and interested in everything. I can think of lots of meetings with little accomplished, but never with such memories.

The industry continued to beckon, and despite having passed my eightieth birthday, I went ahead and produced one final film as a result of the apparent great interest in the 100th anniversary of the end of World War I. The film tells the story of one of the first Americans killed in that war.

An American martyr, Coldstream Guards Lt. Charles Fletcher Hartley, had been killed in the Battle of Cambrai in France on November 27, 1917. He was the uncle of my good friend and composer Doug Hartley, who served as co-director and musical director for this film. Lt. Hartley had fought prior to America's physical entry into the war. One of the highlights of the film is the centennial commemorative ceremony at his memorial in the village of Fontaine Notre Dame organized by grateful French villagers on November 25, 2017.

Endorsed by the US WWI Centennial Commission, the film played at the Harvard Clubs of DC and Boston in May 2018 and November 2018, shortly after the centennial of the WWI armistice. Very positive media coverage and audience feedback followed.

I wish, after all these years, I could claim I had developed a successful formula for producing films. We produced films somewhat haphazardly and by the seat of our pants, but it was great fun, and a wonderful and educational experience for me.

The truth is, we generally followed our best instincts and did whatever we thought would be necessary to create a film people would enjoy. I don't mind saying I am modestly proud of the films we produced for the goodwill they generated in the production process and, hopefully, for the value they brought to audiences.

It's been a wild and wonderful ride.

Calling on the Dalai Lama in
Dharamshala, India, 2014.

chapter eight

My Passions

After letting go of my childhood passion for cattle-ranching, acquired on a trip to the Arizona mountains as a boy, I eventually fell into two other major extra-curricular pre-occupations. The first was flying. I had always loved the idea of airplanes. I filled my school notebooks with sketches of planes. During World War II, I collected photos and paintings of war planes in action and always expressed the hope that someday I could fly.

This was a dream both my parents did little to encourage, thinking it was foolhardy and dangerous. So nothing ever came of this until I graduated from college, served two years in the military, entered the Foreign Service, and got married—all events that established my identity as an independent person. Once I was a self-sufficient being, and the State Department sent me to my first post overseas, I saw a real opportunity to learn to fly.

There was a French flying club in Dakar, subsidized by the French government, where one could take flying lessons very cheaply. The club had several small Jodel trainer aircraft and even an old stunt biplane that could be used for instruction. I never got into stunt flying (I did make smart decisions once in a while).

I threw myself wholeheartedly into this new passion to break the bonds of the earth and took regular and frequent lessons. After several months, I had accumulated the skills and flying time to qualify for the private pilot examination. It was a thrill to pass and become a French-African licensed private pilot.

I have to admit my great admiration for my wife, Elizabeth, during this time. I know she was scared of the whole thing, as my parents had been, but Elizabeth never complained and always supported me. A true brave spouse, she even accompanied me from time to time and let me take the kids for little trips. My father was also keen on flying with me, and maybe even a bit envious.

I was indebted to Talmage Butler, an American flying missionary who had a plane and regularly flew mercy missions out of his missionary station deep in the interior of Senegal. I flew with him as often as I could and learned much about flying at his knee. He always let me do the flying. Each time before we took off, he crossed himself. That bothered me a bit, until eventually I realized he did that every time he took off, even when he was the pilot.

I also learned of the inherent risks of bush flying, which Talmage often had to take if he was to fulfill his responsibilities to help his fellow man. I remember clearly one event that occurred when Talmage was flying far in the interior to help in the construction of a medical clinic.

He was supposed to fly some material out of this village. There was a lot to carry, and he knew it would put his plane over its weight limits. But he knew his plane very well and was pretty sure he would not have a problem taking off from the small airfield. His trick in such instances was to turn on the retracting mechanism for his landing gear while he was gathering speed down the runway to take off. As the plane gained speed and air buoyancy, weight would gradually be taken off the landing gear, it would retract, and the sudden reduced drag would make him airborne.

Unfortunately, he had not noticed the tall jungle grass growing at the end of this dirt runway. As he sped down the runway, he indeed did start to become airborne, but the underside of his aircraft struck the high grass. As it brushed against the plane, it created static electricity. The plane strained but could not break that electric bond. It gradually settled back down to earth. The partially withdrawn undercarriage was wrecked, his propeller twisted and bent. End of flight, but luckily there was no personal injury.

The story had a happy ending. The French were very cognizant of the good work Talmage and his plane did in serving remote communities that could not be reached otherwise. Their air force stepped in, helped him get the plane back to Dakar, then took it up to Morocco where they fixed the damage and made it like new again. It was touching to me what the French did, helping a fellow pilot in distress. I was happy as an embassy employee to help him maneuver through the inevitable bureaucratic entanglements.

When flying the bush country with Talmage, I had to be prepared for anything and do my best to avoid calamity. It didn't always have to do directly with flying. Once Talmage flew my father (who was visiting), the deputy chief of mission, and me way into the interior of Senegal, where few ventured. It was rumored that a cannibal tribe still survived back there, although they had given up the practice of cannibalism. I was told that every seven years they had big initiation ceremonies with lots of dancing and rituals. So, of course, it seemed important to witness that. Talmadge agreed to fly us there since he, too, was curious.

Off we went. It entailed the two-hour flight to Talmage's mission, followed by three hours by Jeep, deep into the back country (Jeep courtesy of Talmage again, of course).

About an hour short of our destination, we crossed paths with another Jeep, which desperately waved us down. They were carrying a person in urgent need of medical help. It was so lucky for them that Talmage was with us, for he immediately clambered out of his Jeep, gave the wheel to a young African colleague of his who was traveling with us, and climbed into the Jeep going the other way to fly the poor soul to a hospital. He assured us the young African was

Learning to fly in Dakar.

a responsible driver and would take us to the ceremonies and bring us back. So we continued on our way, regretfully leaving Talmage behind.

We got to the ceremonies and settled down to watch. We noticed an armed guard, which gave us confidence; he was surely there to make sure the tribe, in a fit of religious fervor, did not revert to old practices. The ceremonies started and there was lots of hopping around and chanting. Then, suddenly, it stopped. After much discussion among the tribal people, the armed guard came over to us.

"Sorry," he said. "They cannot continue with their ceremony with outsiders around—you have to leave."

It was a terrible disappointment, but what could we do? By then it was probably close to midnight, and we had no choice except to climb back into our Jeep and head for Talmage's mission. Off we went, in the dead of night, the young African in charge of driving.

We must have driven for at least an hour when the Jeep coughed, hiccupped and died. My God! What to do? Nothing but empty tundra all around, miles from even an African hut, wild animals out there, maybe even lions.

Well, there was nothing to do. The young African was the only one who did not seem perturbed; his advice was to stay near the Jeep and try to catch some sleep, which is what he promptly did. There being no alternative, we did our best to follow suit. We all thought we heard lions, but I doubt it, in retrospect.

In subsequent trips around Africa's untamed wilderness, I observed that if you were in a truck or car, even one with a retractable roof, you could get within literally a few feet of a lion or some other wild animal, and it paid absolutely no attention to you. You could practically reach out and touch them (not recommended!). We once even came across a male and a female lion deeply engrossed in each other, and we might as well have been on Mars for all the attention they paid us.

Finally, dawn broke. With daylight, we gathered some stones to spell out the word "GAS" in big letters on the dirt road surface. We settled down to wait, but never saw a soul. After what seemed like an eternity, we heard the distant sound of an aircraft. It was

Talmage! We waved wildly, he circled us, then scooted back in the direction he came from.

Not too long after, a bus full of people stopped by, the first and only sign of life we had seen since the evening before. There proceeded lots of talk and gesticulation between our driver, the bus driver, and all its passengers, then everyone was back on the bus and off it went.

Not too long after that, a Jeep came careening down the dirt road—Talmage! He found that the fuel line on our Jeep had somehow shaken loose over the rough road, and all the fuel had drained out. He had seen our sign and so was loaded with gas, and he knew exactly how to fix the Jeep. Soon we were headed back to his mission and safety. End of adventure.

I think everyone was particularly in awe of my seventy-year-old father for having taken it all with considerable aplomb. He certainly had a great story to tell his diplomatic friends.

I remember once our temporary chief of mission needed to go to Nouakchott, the brand-new capital of newly independent Mauretania. The country hardly had any towns or infrastructure, just a vast expanse of the Sahara desert with scattered nomadic settlements and occasional remnants of a French military presence. To be independent, the citizens needed a capital. So the Mauritanians selected a spot near the Atlantic coastline and started building Nouakchott.

The US made plans to build an embassy with appropriate housing for staff. Those of us in Dakar were duly accredited there, and I eagerly volunteered to be with the first contingent of officers to actually live in Nouakchott. The Department accepted the idea, and one senior officer, Pierre Graham, and I were going to represent the US in that remote location as soon as housing could be built.

Until then, we "covered" Mauretania out of the embassy in Dakar. This made it important that periodic trips be taken to Nouakchott to show the flag and deal with the new government. What better way to take such trips than via Talmadge's always-enthusiastic offer of assistance? Such an official mission would require a co-pilot, or so I convinced the powers that be.

So there I was flying with Talmage and our charge d'affaires to

My flying companion and good friend
Talmage Butler refueling in Nouakchott,
Mauretania. Standing in the front is an
airport guard.

Nouakchott for an official visit. The charge, also an adventurous sort, took advantage of the occasion to drop in on Boutilimit, a small former outpost of the French Foreign Legion further out in the Sahara. This was true adventure, and I loved it, as I think Talmadge and the charge did, too.

All went well on our official stop in the capital and the detour to Boutilimit. Distances were substantial, so we needed to refuel in Nouakchott on our return voyage. It had an official airport and air services, according to the charts. When we landed, there was much bustling around, confusion, and embarrassment on the part of the ground crew. Sirs, we were told, most unfortunately the airport is out of gas.

Horrors. We had visions of being stuck there for who knew how long until a new shipment of fuel arrived. All that was available was ordinary gas to refuel trucks working in the area.

Bush pilot Talmage, after some thought, came up with a possible solution—if we were willing to go along with it. He was fairly sure his plane could fly on the low-grade truck gas. It was not good for his engine, but he thought it could survive the hour or so it would take us to get back to Dakar. Talmage would take off using the aviation fuel he still had in his tanks. Then, once airborne at altitude, he would shift to the tank holding truck fuel. Flying slowly, that would get us close enough to Dakar that he then could shift back to the remaining aviation fuel to assure a safe landing. We looked at each other, shrugged, and agreed to the plan. We had little choice!

We took off without a hitch, got to altitude, dialed back the engine, and flew without a problem to Dakar. Switching over to the remaining aviation fuel, we landed safely and nonchalantly. And his engine suffered no harm.

When my wife and I ended our tour in Dakar and returned to Washington, I was sad to say good-bye to Talmage and his charming wife and little son. They continued their missionary work in their remote corner of Senegal, providing life-saving services to the indigenous population and surely feeling that they were saving souls as well. To Talmage's enormous credit, he never once spoke to me about religion, allowing our friendship to flourish on the basis of a shared love of flying and a shared American nationality.

It was a number of years later, after we had already gone on to other assignments, that the news reached us: Talmage and family were killed in a plane crash. His mission had decided he needed a new plane after all those years of flying his old Beechcraft Bonanza. While he was on home leave with his family, they authorized him to shop around. He heard of what seemed a perfect replacement available in southern Florida, so he and his family went there to test fly the aircraft. They took off and headed out over the Atlantic for some test maneuvers and never came back. The disappearance was attributed to a disturbance created by the Bermuda triangle.

To me, he will always be one of the true heroes I met in my lifetime. May he and his family rest in peace.

After my wife and I returned to the US, I was able to continue my interest in flying. Thanks to the GI Bill, I was able to take advanced aviation training. I first obtained my commercial flying certificate (I could fly for pay), then my instrument rating (I could fly by reference to instruments only) and, finally, my certificate as a flight instructor.

For several years thereafter I thoroughly enjoyed this extracurricular activity as a kind of half-career, working during the week in the State Department and on weekends at the local airport teaching others to fly. When I went to Guatemala as a political officer, the country recognized my private pilot's certificate, so I was able to keep on flying as a pastime there.

Flying in Guatemala was fun, but as a diplomat, I could not teach. The rugged, mountainous terrain with the Caribbean on one side and the Pacific on the other made for nice weekend flying to the beach or up into the highlands where the colorfully dressed Indian population resided.

Back in Washington DC, I gave lessons regularly, and the income from the lessons permitted me to buy my own aircraft. When the department transferred me to Canada, I could have kept on flying, but not for pay, which I needed if I wanted to continue the activity. I had gotten too advanced, I guess, and puddle-jumping did not hold too much attraction. I sold my plane, a very sad moment for me, and the end of an important part of my life.

What next? It took a little time, but I began to look at other activities that held interest. One of these was sailing. Our vacation home in Vermont was on a small lake, and it was easy to buy what amounted to a glorified surfboard with a mainsail and foresail to go up and down the lake's length. That way I learned the basics about hoisting sails, tacking, coming about, etc. It was a lot of fun. If a gust of wind tipped me over, so what? Just get it upright again.

Very quickly I yearned for a bigger boat, which would allow longer trips on the Chesapeake Bay and more exploration and experimentation. Soon I had a twenty-four-foot cabin cruiser, followed by a thirty-foot Catalina, which fit the bill perfectly. Then some friends invited me to sail the eastern seaboard and venture onto the high seas. Things were getting more interesting.

Real sailing meant open-ocean sailing. For that, I decided, a thirty-five footer was needed. It was big enough to handle the high seas, but not so big that you were suddenly burdened by more complex mechanisms and more likely to need crew. After much shopping around, I settled for a thirty-five-foot Freedom, a slightly unusual boat because it had an extra-large mainsail and huge mast with a relatively small foresail. The mast was of carbon fiber, which made it extra strong. It was also easier to sail solo, since the rigging was simpler. Now I drew the line—nothing bigger.

I never had any sailing lessons. I learned by doing and by sailing with more accomplished sailors who were always glad to instruct. After a number of years, I was a reasonably competent sailor. I might not win races, but I could handle bad weather and unknown locations where one had to rely on charts and instruments. I never hesitated to sail wherever I wanted, from the Chesapeake Bay, where I got my start, to the western Canadian seaboard, our eastern seaboard from homebase down through the Caribbean and the Panama Canal (on a friend's boat), the coasts of Vietnam and southeast Asia, and African and Mediterranean coastal waters. I knew enough not to challenge the weather, that's for sure, and had no problem retreating to safe harbors to await better forecasts.

The first trip I took on my new Freedom was to enter the Bermuda Regatta, which meant sailing from the Chesapeake Bay to Bermuda and back. It doesn't seem like much, but it was true ocean sailing. As crew I had a good friend, who was a professional navy officer, and his wife, and my daughter Patti, who bravely accompanied me. It was so nice and exciting to actually have a member of my family with me! My other two daughters and my wife were not so keen on sailing. They gladly joined me for occasional sails around the Bay, but not more.

On this trip, we ran into some heavy seas that delayed our arrival in Bermuda by two days for a total ocean voyage of six days. This caused my wife some consternation; she had flown ahead to meet us and began to worry when we did not show up on time. But we had a good time in Bermuda and an uneventful sail back. Patti had to fly back because of her schedule, but a very nice young man, a friend of daughter Tina's from high school days, joined us.

I took several trips up and down the eastern seaboard as crew for friends and had one truly memorable trip from the Chesapeake all the way down to the Bahamas, through those islands, then out into the open ocean to cross the Caribbean to the Panama Canal. I remember passing through some enormous swells; the boat would struggle to the top, then plunge into the trough, losing sight of the ocean on either side. But the boat handled it all beautifully, and it was an exciting trip.

I particularly recall all the wonderful night sailing (when weather was good): starry skies, the moon shining brightly, phosphorescent ocean slipping by, the rustle of waves against the sides, beautiful and peaceful. As helmsman on duty, I was the only person on deck— wonderful solitude. Then dawn, the sun slowly rising, perfection.

All this inspired self-confidence enough to take up chartering around the world. Time was precious and responsibilities made it hard to take too much time off, but I could hop a plane to Thailand or elsewhere and enjoy some of the most beautiful tropical seas on a chartered boat.

We sailed this way several times in Thailand, once exactly a year before the huge tsunami of December 2004, when at least

4,812 people were killed. The man who had taken us scuba diving at Phuket the prior year was killed, along with one of his children. His dive shop where we had rented our equipment was destroyed. I went back a few months after the tsunami to see if we could help. It was so sad—a scene of total devastation—but inspirational to see how the Thai people were reacting to the tragedy. A very gentle but very tough people.

Chartering proved to be a very nice way to sail and see the world. There are large, reputable worldwide organizations willing to charter almost any size boat from twelve to sixty feet or more, if you can show you have the skills. My family chartered in Vietnam, Polynesia, Croatia, Canada, the Bahamas and the Caribbean, the San Juan Islands, and sometimes just locally. All was most wonderful, adventurous and satisfying, a relaxing pastime and good skill to have. We all became avid scuba divers.

Sailing became a true passion, and it was with great regret when I had to withdraw from the activity. My daughters had drifted away, my wife never really was enthusiastic, and I found myself doing more and more solo sailing. It was fun, but I missed the companionship of sailing. I finally sold my boat. I was in my late seventies, and it was getting harder and harder to do all the things required for such undertakings. A boat is a lot of work, much of it enjoyable, but eventually tiring to do alone.

The Arctic and Antarctic have long been a source of fascination for me. This began during a foreign service assignment from 1972 to 1976, when I ended up in Ottawa as a political officer. One of my responsibilities was to report on the Arctic region. The US government was nervous about the neighbors to the north and over the Pole—the Soviet Union—and wondered how vulnerable we would be to encroachments by them.

An enormous amount of money was spent in the late fifties to construct the DEW (Distant Early Warning) Line, a series of radar stations all across the barren frozen Canadian and US north manned by radar technicians and others. This was a very lonely and remote assignment: six months of darkness in winter (temperatures often fifty degrees below freezing) and six months of relative warmth (maybe thirty degrees).

Along with the construction of the DEW Line, the 1957 North American Air Defense Agreement placed the air forces of Canada and the United States under joint command. Its name was later changed to the North American Aerospace Defense Command, but it kept the NORAD acronym. Our embassy sent me as escort officer for a large US congressional delegation traveling to the Arctic as part of this agreement.

Of equal importance was the construction of the trans-Alaska pipeline (1975–1977), built to supply the lower forty-eight with the huge quantities of oil discovered off the north coast of Alaska, around Prudhoe Bay. It was an enormous undertaking to drill for and exploit oil discovered deep in the Arctic Ocean, under tons of ice, and then build hundreds of miles of oil pipeline. The pipe needed to span the entire state of Alaska down to the Pacific, across open plains, high mountain ranges, and frozen rivers.

The Arctic is a barren place, but huge herds (hundreds of thousands) of animals survive and thrive by marching across the north, seeking seasonal changes in edibles and temperature. Such a huge, human-built pipeline, ten to twenty feet high, and hundreds of miles long, would effectively block caribous' migratory passage, potentially killing entire herds.

This issue was hotly debated. The pipeline people argued the herds would figure something out; the environmentalists called this wishful thinking. To the credit of both sides, they agreed to try an experiment. For every few miles of pipeline, they would construct land bridges up and over it. Would it work?

Everyone waited and watched tensely for the arrival of the first herds. Apparently, they all came to a screeching halt when they reached the pipeline. Then, gingerly, a few sniffed the bridges, pawed the ground, and inched their way up, over, and down the other side. Then they lowered their heads and went on their way. The rest slowly followed. Hallelujah.

My first visit to the Arctic was to Prudhoe Bay in northern Alaska, the headquarters for the large oil exploration and construction that was under way at the time. It was a huge, open space frozen solid with snow and ice, a forbidding scene particularly in the darkness of night. In daylight, the snow would shimmer and glisten, the sky often light and blue (in summer!), the air so clear and clean.

It was a fairly large community composed of numerous buildings linked by heated passageways. There were dormitories, a small hotel, recreation halls, a large dining hall, and a landing strip—a whole little community living unto itself. Everything inside was heated and comfortable.

If a plane landed or took off, it could not turn off its engine until it had been stored in a heated hanger. If left outside for even a few minutes, it would freeze and become useless. If you chose to walk around a bit, Arctic clothing was extremely bulky, but it did keep you warm as long as you kept moving.

I was usually visiting as a US embassy rep from Ottawa, and the local population, ranging from native peoples to radar and other technicians, was gracious in showing me their exploratory wells, their oil rigs, and the storage silos. They even took me on a short flight around the area.

One time I hitched a ride on a plane used to fly supplies and individuals to and from our bases in the north country. I was returning from a visit to Dawson, Alaska, a major terminal for the Alaska pipeline. I had gone up there simply because the pipeline had become so controversial, and the embassy wanted to know what was going on. We were encountering considerable criticism from the Canadians, mostly on environmental matters.

It was a military DC-3, very informal, with the pilot cabin door open. We weren't more than eight or ten passengers. As a pilot, I naturally hung around the cabin and eavesdropped, which they didn't seem to mind. I looked out the window and noticed a thin layer of ice accumulating on the wing; the pilot evidently noticed it at the same time, for the wing de-icers were suddenly at work. These are like large rubber balloons attached to the leading edge of the wing.

When turned on, the balloons quickly start to inflate, theoretically causing the ice accumulation on the wing to crack and break off.

This worked at first, but one could see the battle was being lost. Ice accumulated faster than the de-icers removed it. The pilot radioed anxiously to air traffic control and requested a change of altitude where the temperature would work for us by warming the wing. Permission was immediately granted, and the pilot went to work, playing with the de-icing equipment and making the plane do some dancing up and down.

I could see large slabs of ice sliding off the wing, the plane regained stability, and in a few moments we burst out of the clouds and into sunshine! You could hear a muffled sigh of relief and praise for the pilot. I learned that such occurrences were not so unusual in this new environment; you had to live with it.

For all the inherent risk, I must confess that nothing moved my romantic heart so much as flying in the Arctic at night beneath a star-filled sky. Occasional shooting stars appeared in the huge black sky. The vast and empty snow-covered landscape of plains and high mountains lay below. The only sound was the muffled purr of the aircraft engine.

One of my greatest joys was the result of my good fortune to be a licensed pilot and flight instructor. When taking off on a trip across the Arctic in a small aircraft—mostly single-engine four-to-six-passenger craft—the pilot in charge might ask if anyone on board was also a pilot. "*And how!*" I would practically bellow. I would be designated co-pilot pro-tem and was allowed to fly the plane in this winter wonderland. I must add in honesty that this happened quite rarely, but the memory remains with me forever.

There are a number of stories about the Arctic that *can* curl your hair. A rescue pilot flew to a remote corner where a woman was having severe labor pains and needed to be evacuated to a hospital. He picked her up in his plane and started to fly back to his base on the DEW Line.

Unfortunately, as often happens up there, the weather turned very nasty very quickly. Soon the pilot found himself in the midst of snow and ice. The plane crashed. He survived, but she was severely injured and died. Home base sent out search planes to try to find him, but several days of fruitless efforts resulted in no success, and eventually the search was called off. The assumption was that they had been killed.

For three months the pilot survived alone in his wrecked airplane in the middle of the frozen terrain of the Arctic. He had supplies that lasted him a while, but eventually he had nothing. He could melt ice to drink but had no food for sustenance. So he ate parts of his passenger. It was either that or die.

This sounds like a horrible choice, and indeed it was, but one must consider the environment.

The local native population had long ago accepted cannibalism as a necessary fact of life if one wanted to survive. They had been doing it over centuries. They understood the powerful need to survive and how horrible death in the Arctic could be. For a Western-raised and educated person to resort to the practice was a horrible repudiation of everything he had been taught, an incredibly brave and counter-cultural thing to do.

I was visiting the DEW Line station when they finally found the rescue pilot. They put him in the room next to mine. These stations were remarkably isolated and lonely places. You could see them easily: a big, round radar dome on top of a small cluster of buildings, and not too far off, a landing strip. Then vast open spaces.

Most of the stations were on Canadian territory, built by the US and manned by personnel from both countries. Since we were primarily responsible for them, it was imperative that US officials such as me keep track of them by visiting once in a while. They were linked by modern technology and communications, so when an accident occurred, the DEW Line station could act as a site for awaiting further evacuation.

While this rescue pilot was housed with us at the station, everyone kept their mouths shut and tried to act normal. I felt enormously sorry for him and eventually understood the horrible alternatives he faced. I could not hold it against him; it was the law of the Arctic.

Of equal fascination to me also is the incredible history of the region. Sir John Franklin (1786–1847) of the British Royal Navy disappeared on his last expedition attempting to chart and navigate the Northwest Passage with two ships, the *Terror* and the *Erebus*. The ships were caught in a storm and became trapped in ice for several years near Prince of Wales Island. Many succumbed to disease, and Franklin finally decided their only hope was to walk to southern Canada.

Only several decades later were their bodies found a hundred miles away. Being good Englishmen, among the supplies they dragged with them were all their dress uniforms, their fine china and cutlery, and other essential equipment! Evidence suggests that they, too, resorted to cannibalism to survive but ultimately all died from exposure. Their two ships were finally discovered two centuries later, frozen solid in the ice, in 2014 and 2016.

Historically, the original explorers treated the very scant native population with haughty disregard. It is now readily accepted that if it hadn't been for the arrogant disregard of the natives by the explorers, many more would have survived. In fact, the famous explorer Alexander Mackenzie thought he was on his death bed in a small hut his team had built for survival. As he lay there breathing what he was sure was his last breath, there was a knock on the door and in walked a native. The man saved his life.

By the time I began visiting the Arctic, native populations resided in their own communities and sometimes worked as casual labor for foreigners. Relations between natives and newcomers appeared friendly, and I recall that we made an effort to help and work with these small groups of native peoples.

Visiting these extremely remote and historic locations gave me the chills, especially when thinking about what the early explorers must have gone through. On one occasion touring DEW Line stations we landed on a remote beach. We joked and teased our British colleagues when staff members from the British contingent appeared and proceeded to set a table with forks and knives for our picnic.

Having explored the North Pole, how could I go on without at least visiting the other end of the world? It, too, had a fascination. My wife and I took a trip to Antarctica in 2004, sailing on the

110-passenger ship, the *Endeavor*. Unfortunately, the US government did not sponsor these trips.

The South Pole greeted us with huge icebergs all over, distant mountains, and vast plains of ice and snow. It seemed much more civilized than the Arctic: lots of people (relatively, of course) and large animal populations. One everlasting memory for me is the huge fields of penguins and flocks of birds—albatrosses, hawks, cormorants, eagles, and others. Whole animal cultures survive in these barren lands, including sea lions, walruses, and whales.

We actually witnessed a leopard sea lion hunt and eat its prey: It sneaked up on a penguin, leapt on it to grab its throat, then, with a vicious toss of its head, killed the animal. The sea lion chewed a bit on the carcass, then took the body in its jaws and violently shook it until the flesh came flying out of its skin. Voilà. Dinner was served.

We also found a greater variety of human settlements—stations belonging to America, Norway, Russia, Sweden, Poland, Greenland, Canada, and Finland. Compared to the Arctic, where nations clearly claim contiguous land, the land in Antarctica is not owned by any one nation, which creates more international competition.

The trip was thoroughly enjoyable and educational, with stops at research stations, abandoned early explorer camps, and the site where Robert F. Scott established his base as he sought to be the first to reach the South Pole. He apparently reached the pole a scant few days after the Norwegian explorer Roald Amundsen. To his enormous disappointment, he found Amundsen's marker already there. On the trip back to his base camp, he and his team ran into really bad weather. He ended up with only three or four survivors in one tent where they huddled together waiting for a break in the storm.

Scott kept a diary and reported that at one moment, one of the four quietly hoisted himself to his feet and announced he was going to step outside for a second. He closed the tent flap behind him and was not seen again. Scott's diary reports the event very briefly. A few days later, when the weather did lift and search parties went looking for the team, they came across the tent with its frozen inhabitants. The last body was found not far from the tent, under a snow bank.

Apparently, tourism in Antarctica has become a real problem.

Ever larger cruise vessels, some with hundreds if not thousands of tourists, pour out of their ships onto the fragile landscape. In a side attraction for the hardier tourists, ships drop anchor in shallow bays during the summer so passengers can take a quick dip in the ocean (presumably so that they can say they did it). My understanding is that successful efforts are being made to limit tourism, which has really become a threat to the environment.

Even more ominous is the fact that global warming is melting ice so rapidly that the arctic regions are ever more accessible. Tour ships are already advertising circumnavigating North America. In my humble opinion, outsiders entering this very fragile part of the world should be highly regulated. It is naïve to think a campground built by explorers a hundred years ago will remain chaste if hordes of tourists armed with cameras descend upon it, unless there are strict controls.

I think of myself as having been so fortunate to have glimpsed the area at a time when things were only beginning to change. I have nothing but admiration for the local native inhabitants who adapted and survived, thrived, and actually created a remarkable culture of their own under the direst of circumstances. The earliest explorers, who found themselves struggling to survive, showed incredible toughness. Their greatest impediment may have been not the environment but their cultural inhibitions and reluctance to engage with the native population.

Although no longer sailing my own boats or piloting my own planes, my love of adventure tourism persists. For my eightieth birthday, in 2013, I thought it would be fun for the family to visit the famous Amazon River basin, particularly the upper reaches, much of which are relatively undeveloped. Indigenous tribes still live along its banks, and a little further inland there still exist some truly isolated native habitations.

We signed up for a boat trip on a stretch of river still not too developed for tourist traffic. The flat-bottomed vessel carried about thirty passengers quite comfortably. Our guides took us up the river, eventually tying up to overhanging trees, then onto motorized canoes along increasingly narrow and shallow streams that flowed into the parent river. We saw occasional wild animals—sloths and caimans, a variety of monkeys, countless birds, fish, and aquatic life, including many piranhas. Snakes, tarantulas, and a wide variety of extremely poisonous frogs were present, too, and one always had to be careful where one walked.

A bit unnerving was the presence of armed policemen on each boat. We were told this was to discourage bandits from sneaking onboard at night, while we were tied up to the trees, and robbing the passengers. The thieves would be long gone back in the jungle before any effective outside help could be summoned, so armed policemen were de rigeur.

We went swimming in the river at one point after being reassured we were in a piranha-free stretch. The river regularly changed color, usually from a ruddy brown to a pitch black. They stopped the boat and told us we could swim when we hit a particularly large chunk of black water. The fish apparently can't tolerate the black water and stay well clear of it. In we went, and it was true. Trust the natives; they know whereof they speak.

It was an unforgettable trip into a different world. The sheer beauty and vastness of the ever-present jungle towering above us, the sounds of animals and birds, the peace and tranquility, the beauty of the vegetation, unspoiled by humans, and the meandering river and its tributaries were just incredible.

I was the only casualty. A large local ant thought I looked tasty. Wow, did that bite hurt! The locals immediately put some salve on the bite and in not too many minutes, the pain subsided. For a brief while, I was sure I was a goner despite reassurances (and probably some discreet local chuckles) that it was "just" a local ant bite.

On this trip I saw that one of my passions has definitely been passed on to the next generation(s). My kids and grandkids enjoy our family trips as much now as when they were younger. This travel legacy, for lack of a better word, was been wonderful for all of us.

Boating on the Peruvian Amazon with
Liz and the girls.

We have shared within our family so many unique experiences that bind us together.

The love of travel, the adventure of going to new places, immersing myself in foreign cultures and customs has been part of my life for as long as I can remember. That's something I'm proud to see my kids enjoying as much as I do. The oldest grandkids already look forward to traveling on their own, and, indeed, off they go as they get old enough.

I never did get back to my original dream of ranching, although it still seems like a pretty good idea, if somewhat unrealistic for me. As a consolation prize, we have had a home in very rural northern Vermont for some forty years. I still love animals. We tried to have a pet dog wherever we were, but that became difficult, as we moved frequently and travelled a lot.

One passion I pursued later in life developed out of my good fortune in business. As I traveled the world and observed so many wonderful people coping with serious challenges, it seemed obvious to me to help where I could. What began as a personal hobby grew into The Ed Nef Foundation.

My three daughters in their early adulthood.

Back row left to right: Liz, Tina, Patricia, and Ed;
middle row left to right: Stefanie and Dave;
front row left to right: Andrew, Emily, Abigail,
and Thomas in the Bahamas.

chapter nine

Starting a Foundation

Thoughts of helping others were bred into me from early on. Throughout my youth, my parents' charity work was ever-present. My mom devoted a great deal of time during the war to helping Polish refugees wherever they were. She also volunteered for the Red Cross. My dad helped establish a Swiss benevolent society whose goal was to assist Swiss in the US suffering from difficult circumstances. This became the primary way for Swiss expatriates living in the US to help their less-fortunate compatriots.

My high school, Phillips Academy at Andover, gave me great impetus in this direction. Its overriding motto, drilled into us, was *non sibi*, not for oneself. The spirit of this motto certainly inspired me in later years: Help others when you can. Another Andover grad, President George H.W. Bush ('42), said, "There can be no definition of a successful life that does not include service to others." Thoughts such as these were guiding principles for me as I grew fortunate enough to have resources I could share.

Operating language schools gave me opportunities to visit and get to know foreign countries, peoples, and cultures that would otherwise not have been easily accessible. This proved to be a pivotal factor in my introduction to a career in charitable giving. I had also witnessed great poverty during my foreign service life in Senegal and throughout Central and South America. One could not cross a street in Dakar without being accosted by disfigured lepers, begging for money.

While one could become a bit inured to the pitiful conditions suffered by many, it still left a lasting impression of how fortunate we are. It was inevitable as I encountered native peoples, often living at subsistence levels, earning as little as a couple hundred dollars a year, that I would also observe the tragedies and hardships that could not be avoided in their circumstances. Their only hope was that something would bring them to the attention of an interested observer.

Of great influence on me was my experience in Mongolia. It was hard not to be impressed by the poverty—in our terms—of the bulk of Mongolia's rural population and their incredible resilience and toughness. They survived under the most difficult conditions.

Imagine living in an animal-skin tent (*ger*), several family members together, heated by one central fire fed by dried animal dung that is accumulated in the warmer weather to be used in the winter. The food is what can be butchered from their small herds of sheep or goats. They might supplement their diet with milk from their animals and perhaps a few hardy vegetables such as potatoes, all boiled in a big pot over the central fire. Outside temperatures often hover around negative thirty or forty degrees.

Never do any of these people beg for assistance. In fact, if you approach one of their *gers*, their immediate reaction is to throw open the flap and invite you in to share their humble meal. In many other parts of Asia, rural populations are often similarly tough and family-oriented.

I undertook my first charitable endeavor as a personal project in Mongolia. Bilguun was a child of a nomadic family I had met during one of my trips to their territory, and I could not help but notice her severely handicapped situation as she crawled around the dirt floor of their *ger*. She was born with a seriously deformed hip, and it was obviously very difficult for the family, who lived off the land.

I wanted to help this girl with corrective surgery. Bilguun's plight aroused sympathy from other donors, too: the Mel Gibson Foundation paid for her airfare, and a very generous pediatric surgeon at the Shriners' Hospital for Children in Los Angeles took her under his wing. She underwent numerous surgeries to correct her hip and was in that city for more than half a year. It seemed like a success.

But soon after she returned to her family, she began having great pains in her hip. What was wrong? The doctor was very distressed and began asking questions about her life in Mongolia. It turned out that as nomads, they often moved around, crossing steppes, forests, and rivers—bingo! The rivers were fast flowing and very cold. The doctor had left inside her bone some of the pins he had placed to help the healing process. When the cold river water hit her leg, the metallic pins would turn very cold and cause terrible pain.

The doctor was very apologetic and explained he usually left the pins inside since they helped strengthen the leg, but they were not essential to the healing process. Of course, most of his patients were from Southern California and never had to contend with freezing water as they forded country streams.

He insisted she return to California. He removed the pins, and the pains never returned. The family was so grateful. They did have to wait patiently for several weeks as Bilguun regained fluency in Mongolian (and forgot her recently learned English).

The experience with Bilguun's family gave me the inspiration I needed to formally create The Ed Nef Foundation, a small 501(c)(3). In no time, I came across another very worthy cause back in my old stomping grounds of Senegal. While my crew and I were there filming a documentary, I met an ambitious and very bright woman named Doussou Konate who had managed to put herself through school and obtain a degree in electrical engineering. I believe she was the first woman in Senegal, if not in all Africa, to achieve such a degree.

Her dream was to bring electric power to the forgotten rural countryside, where electricity was basically nonexistent. A large French electric company provided Dakar and some of the larger communities with electric power it generated using their power grid. But if a site was not readily accessible, as was the case for a good part of Senegal, forget about it.

Several non-profit organizations were already working on this issue in their particular fields of expertise. Tostan, created by a very competent American woman named Molly Melching, was already well-known. Molly did much in education, women's rights, and health. She encouraged locals to undertake various projects, and Doussou took her up on the idea.

After starting her project, Doussou ran out of money and did not have the resources to obtain high-powered renewable batteries. Her village, which had been the beneficiary of her initiative, was suddenly growing dark. There was no light for children to do their homework, no power to help in agricultural projects or medical care. The village was slowly regressing.

The decision was simple. I agreed to make this an objective of my newly established foundation. My very bright executive director, Meiyue (May) Zhou, had a history of working for foundations and non-profits both in the US and China. She proved invaluable in guiding me in this new direction.

We supplied Doussou with the equipment she so desperately needed. It was heartening to observe the enthusiasm of the people in the town as power was gradually restored. Kids could do their homework in the evening, schools could stay open longer, and ordinary business activities were not tied to the rising and setting of the sun.

Back in Mongolia, we kept in touch with Bilguun. She never forgot her experience, and from the moment she settled back in Mongolia, she vowed to become an English teacher in her home country. Now with the support of my foundation, we helped to pay for her education.

She has consistently studied English in Mongolia to the extent that was at all possible. The lady who bought my school (Santis Educational Services) in Ulaan Baatar, Ms. Orgilmaa Doloonjin, arranged a training program for Bilguun at SES where she was able to undertake English studies during her summer vacation in 2016.

Julia Clark, a wonderful lady who came to Mongolia on a Fulbright scholarship to work with indigenous peoples, offered another summer opportunity. She employed Bilguun as an aide at her archaeological field-camp where she could practice her English. Bilguun graduated from high school, and in the fall of 2017 she enrolled in the Mongolian State University of Education English Department. She is off and running to achieve her life goal.

Eventually, we hope to bring her to the US to help her achieve English proficiency and thereby add another dedicated teacher of English to the very small roster now in existence in Mongolia.

My affection and fascination with Mongolia continued to point me in that direction, and I quickly found other opportunities to help. One came from Bruno Frohlich, a brilliant research scholar with the Smithsonian National Museum of Natural History, a professor at Dartmouth, and a good friend. Bruno told me about a project of his where local herdsmen discovered an underground cave in the southern Mongolian Gobi Desert in 2004. The possibility of human remains was reported, so a team from the Mongolian Academy of Sciences and the Smithsonian Institution came to investigate. They found ten human mummified bodies, all in very good to excellent condition, which were sent to the Smithsonian.

What interested me greatly (so I am a bit morbid!) was Bruno's report that ten individuals were involved: four adults, three adolescents and three infants less than a year old. He wrote that the cause of death was strangulation, garroting, and/or hanging. "In three cases the ropes used in the killings were still tightly wrapped around the necks, and later CT scanning showed fractured cervical vertebrae."

The DNA analyses showed family ties among some of the human remains. Radiometric dating from rope and skin tissue places them between AD 1300 and AD 1470, corresponding to the end of the Great Mongolian Empire, a time of cultural upheaval.

Support for the project was provided by The Mongolian Academy of Sciences, the Smithsonian Institution, and The Ed Nef Foundation. I am proud that we were able to help Bruno logistically in

Young Mongolian Tsaatan reindeer herder
Bilguun after her operation.

Doussou Konate, a solar engineer in rural Senegal, receiving new solar batteries from our foundation.

executing this ground-breaking exploration. What he found and reported on is truly fascinating and educationally profound.

This was one of the twenty-two projects the foundation assisted in nine countries, including the US. Almost half were undertaken in Mongolia or for Mongolian communities in the US. This included helping The Mongolian School of the National Capital Area in Washington as it tried to develop a circus-training program. In Mongolian culture, circus activity is a highly esteemed profession and looked up to with admiration. We also helped the school compile its own textbooks under the able leadership of the school director.

The Ed Nef Foundation has funded a number of projects in Africa, in addition to the Americas and Asia, working with such organizations as Youth Education for Development and Entrepreneurship, the Fula Women Association of North America, Tostan in West Africa, Flagstaff International Relief Effort in Mongolia, The Nation Foundation in Uganda, and the Makuyu Education Initiative in Kenya.

We have given scholarships to individuals and helped with the development of several schools in remote corners of the world, such as Uganda, Kenya, Senegal, and Vietnam. We have funded women's education and welfare projects in Cameroon and Zambia. Often, a project came to our attention while we were working in an area under different mandates. For example, our contacts with Tostan occurred as a result of our film project about Senegalese women.

It was bound to happen that eventually I would see my new endeavor of non-profit, documentary film production as a natural complement to my foundation work. A whole country could be influenced in good ways, if one succeeded in making entertaining films to inform and educate a curious audience. Films already played a decisive role in the field of education, and I saw lots of opportunities there.

I produced films not for profit, but to help educate and inform people's opinions about events—the true objective of a genuine foundation. Eventually, my film production company was absorbed into the foundation.

After the foundation became better known, we started receiving requests for cooperation on other projects. For example, the Nation Foundation, a Los Angeles nonprofit, approached us requesting assistance for its educational projects in Uganda. These cooperative efforts turned out to be quite successful. Also, friends and contacts in other organizations, like Bruno Frohlich at the Smithsonian, requested our assistance in South America and Mongolia.

While managing my school in Mongolia, I helped introduce the Smithsonian to the world of Mongolian natural history, anthropology and archeology, which ultimately became a long-term commitment by the institution and one of its leaders, Bill Fitzhugh. He took a great interest in early historic Mongolian relics, including great finds in the Gobi Desert.

Bill Fitzhugh, in addition to serving on my foundation's board, is the director of Arctic Studies at the Smithsonian National Museum of Natural History. We helped sponsor a Smithsonian Arctic Studies program that attracted audiences of over 7,000, mostly young students from around the United States. The four-day education program in 2015 examined how climate change is affecting the environment in the Arctic area.

Support for my foundation comes primarily from my personal funds. We also receive generous contributions from benevolent donors and organizations. Among them is Fengqi Li, employee of the World Meteorological Organization in Geneva. Thanks to her strong reference, my Foundation received funds from The UN Staff 1% for Development Fund to support our school project in Senegal.

Ed Story, a member of our board, and his daughter Sara were both extremely generous in their support, as were an Andover classmate, Bob Doran, and Selina F. Little and Elizabeth Cross, relatives of Charles Hartley, the hero of our WWI film. Another donor is Andrea Knox, one of a team of *Philadelphia Inquirer* reporters who won the Pulitzer prize in 1980. After leaving the Inquirer, she became the executive director of a non-profit organization, the Chester Children's Chorus, in Pennsylvania. Han Peruzzi, a successful Long & Foster Realtor in Northern Virginia, also made several generous donations to my foundation.

One of our most successful projects was a suggestion from my

*Meiyue (May) Zhou, executive director of our foundation
(left), with foundation attorney Elaine Chang (right).*

daughter Tina to partner with Habitat for Humanity International
to build a house in Zambia for single mom Elizabeth Chupa. In
July 2018, foundation board member Tina Nef (my daughter) and
foundation website designer and cinematographer Roderick Mercer
joined the construction team.

Elizabeth, twenty-two years old, provided for her four siblings
and three children. Her parents had died and her husband left.
Elizabeth earned a living on the streets of Kabwe, Zambia selling
charcoal. When Rod and Tina's team arrived, the local builders
with whom they were to work for the week had already erected the

corners of the building. It was then time to mortar cinderblocks in, leaving room for windows and doors frames.

The crew consisted of fifteen volunteers from the United States, most of them from the Seattle area, a half dozen local craftsmen, and a Habitat coordinator. Elizabeth also worked on the project, hauling blocks and shoveling mortar with her infant strapped to her back.

By the end of the week, the walls and floor were built, the windows and a door installed, and the roof in place. The team had built a three-room home with a covered entry for cooking in the rainy season. The home had no electricity, plumbing, or furniture—typical in Zambia—but it was secure shelter with a locking front door. It is located in a community of several dozen such homes.

On their last day of work, the team decorated the finished home with streamers and balloons. They hired local musicians and held a dedication ceremony to present Elizabeth with the keys to the front door.

Most foundation projects remained small, under $10,000. Often, not much more was needed to put a project over the top. We also supported somewhat larger projects, such as helping build a school, a dining hall or dormitory.

We always worked hard to ascertain the validity of grant requests. For example, one program pleaded with us to help build basketball and volleyball courts for a school. It seemed reasonable enough, but upon further inspection we found that almost nothing had been done to further the project beyond some talk. It was obviously going to be a long time before anything would materialize. We told them to come back when they were more ready.

In recent years, a large-scale prosthetics project in Mongolia has demanded most of our attention and resources. The undertaking will require sustained and substantial funding and effort, but I remain devoted to the idea that few things could be of greater assistance to Mongolia than a facility dedicated to providing amputees with affordable, modern artificial limbs. Life on the steppes can be very hard and risky.

One of the first to receive a prosthetic leg from our foundation was a young man, Munkhochir Dorjsuren, who rounded up wild horses and tamed them for his community. He had first broken his leg taming wild horses far from any village or town with medical facilities. When his leg fractured, the usual remedy was implemented for lack of serious help—amputation. He was given a wooden leg of relatively little use in his tough career. Subsequently, this wooden leg broke.

The poor man was totally crestfallen, his career ambitions to train wild horses (essential means of transportation) seeming to crumble. He persisted despite great adversity and was selected to receive one of the first more modern prosthetic legs from us. Most unfortunately, those who provided it to him never gave him proper training. Sure enough, not long after he returned to his profession, he put too much pressure on the prosthetic, and it broke.

So he was going to get a second chance. A new leg was made for him, his third artificial leg. Strict instruction was given to everyone that the prosthetic was an expensive medical device, not a tool, and it could bear only so much pressure. While he now has the use of two legs, time will tell if he can safely resume his career with horses.

Prosthetics also provided a new avenue for a boy I first met at around the same time as I'd met Bilguun. Enkh-Amar Gantumur, a young boy from a very modest family, was born with two club feet. We brought him to the Shriners' Hospital for Children in Los Angeles where they successfully straightened one of his feet, but the other one could not be helped. The doctor's painful decision was he would be better off if the foot were amputated and he were fitted with a prosthetic device. That worked until Enkh-Amar outgrew that device, and no replacement could be found. He had to turn to a crutch to replace the lost foot.

Enkh-Amar was scheduled to receive a new, larger prosthetic from us but, for reasons beyond our control, the young man had to withdraw from the project. This was a very sad development for us. Fortunately, the first-rate Mongolian crew assisting us on this project went to work and quickly found a highly qualified young girl, Oyundari Gangantaya, to be the candidate.

Then, in a serendipitous turn, I attended my 65th (yes, 65th) class reunion at Phillips Academy in Andover, Mass. I was a bit overwhelmed to see what today's kids are doing in high schools such as Andover. I was brought up with a start when I visited what Andover calls "the Nest." It is an incubator for students to experiment with whatever ideas and interests they might have. One of their tools is 3D-printer technology.

Here students were doing incredible things with the resources at their disposal. These are *kids*, high school students, and this is really high tech stuff. A thought occurred: Could a foot be created with a 3D-printer?

The response of both students and the Nest's inspirational leader, Mike Barker, blew my mind. "Let's give it a try," they said. Hands and other body parts were already being made with 3D-printer technology, but not feet. The challenge with feet is the intricacy of the anatomy and the weight they must bear.

So there they were, high school kids, seizing an incredible opportunity to do some real good in a real situation using very high technology. It was almost like a government foreign aid program without the bureaucracy! Printing Prosthetics @ Phillips Academy was the official name of our project.

We embarked on a project to produce a 3D-printer prosthetic foot for Oyundari, the disabled girl in Mongolia. Then reality overtook us: 3D-printing was producing miracles, but the technology still had a long way to go to produce that very complicated part of the human anatomy, the foot. If we were to produce prosthetics in the short term, we would have to revert to more traditional methods and work at reducing those costs.

So things did not go as planned. But adversity strengthens the soul, right? The project at Phillips Academy, Andover ended after about a year, with a general admission that 3D-printing technology alone could not handle the project. In fairness to Andover, it must have considered such questions as liability and future funding legitimate causes for concern.

The Andover students, under the tutelage of prosthetic manufacturers, eventually created a wonderful prosthetic foot for Oyundari using traditional methods.

A movement is spreading to provide prosthetics to the many

Mongolian contortionist Urangoo.

Mongolians in need, attracting individuals, organizations, and businesses. John Dieli, chief production officer and clinic manager of Hanger, Inc., the largest prosthetics manufacturer in the US, is involved. Mongolians in Mongolia and in the US have rallied as well.

The first objective is to find the means and knowledge to create a model foot suitable for duplication and production using traditional methods and technology available in other parts of the world but not yet in Mongolia. This includes a plan to help develop a facility in Mongolia to make prosthetic devices by whatever means possible to help some of Mongolia's 30,000 individuals who lack limbs and have no resources to buy prosthetics. This will need continuing contributions from interested parties, and, in the long run, the Mongolian government will have to assume responsibility for prosthetic production in Mongolia.

A crucial phase of our prosthetics project was the experimental treatment of five candidates, including the young man who originally sparked my imagination but had to postpone treatment, Enkh-Amar. We located medical facilities, such as work rooms at the hospital and elsewhere, for John to perform his work and train medical personnel to create prosthetic devices.

John accomplished miracles in obtaining all the equipment necessary, donated to the cause by generous US manufacturers, to build prosthetic feet. Then Esu Erdenebat (the daughter of one of my loyal former employees, Aya Choijindorj), who recently graduated in Community Health from George Mason University, became a prime coordinator for this program in Ulaan Baatar. The lead physician at the National Trauma Orthopedic Research Center of Mongolia (Trauma Hospital) happens to be her father, Dr. Erdenebat Khoilogdorj.

A team of American experts, led by John, traveled in May 2018 to Ulaan Baatar with all the necessary supplies to treat the patients for a week. At the same time, key Mongolian technical personnel received training in the process.

The Trauma Hospital in Ulaan Baatar provided support, as did doctors and technical personnel, who all look forward to further training and the eventual establishment of a full-scale facility in the area. Mongolian news media covered our project enthusiastically. Numerous inquiries came from local people throughout the week.

There is much to be done, and we are always running into an incredibly complex bureaucratic structure where it can take forever to achieve very much. The problems of corruption also rear their heads. The goal is to bring the Mongolian government more into the picture so that in the not-too-distant future, the treatment of those in need of prosthetics will be a natural part of the governmental structure.

As I began to wind down the activities of my foundation, I learned the inspiring story of a Mongolian woman, Oyuntsetseg "Ono" Anand, who lost both her legs many years ago in a terrible tragedy. Collaborating with Ono seemed a fitting end to my work with Mongolian amputees.

When she was thirteen, a horse-related accident badly damaged

Ono's leg, and doctors decided to amputate, a typical course of treatment in Mongolia. She was wheeled into the operating room, followed by the surgeon, who no one noticed was inebriated.

When Ono woke up from surgery, she discovered that the surgeon had amputated her good leg. Of course, her injured leg still had to be amputated, so eventually she lost both legs below the knee.

This sort of unbelievable misfortune might easily demolish someone. But not Ono. She and her husband determined to make her life better by turning to prosthetics. They struggled through many hardships, but they succeeded in building a modest but profitable private prosthetic facility.

Just as they could begin to enjoy their accomplishment, Ono's husband died suddenly of a heart attack. She was alone with a child to support and a business to run. She had provided the technical expertise for their prosthetic company, and her husband had brought great business acumen. In his absence, greedy vultures tried to expropriate her hard-earned property. Soon, the State Bank indicated it would repossess her building.

In desperation, Ono appealed to the Prime Minister of Mongolia. The Prime Minister prevented the seizure of her property, but Ono was still deeply in debt.

Orgilmaa Doloonjin, a mutual friend, brought Ono's plight to our attention. The foundation quickly mobilized its resources. One particularly helpful individual was John Dieli, who helped obtain large quantities of donated supplies and equipment for the project. He also enthusiastically agreed to train the Mongolian technicians at Ono's clinic.

We knew that our program could not be a one-shot affair. Mongolia needs the permanent presence of prosthetic professionals and a modernized version of Ono's clinic.

The foundation enlisted the support of a large charity organization, Friends of Mongolia. The former chairman of that organization, US Ambassador Al LaPorta, also threw in his support, as did Galbadrakh Gombosuren, one of the largest film producers in Mongolia, who would like to produce a film about our work with Ono. He is also chairman of United Mongolia, a nonprofit based in Virginia.

Oyuntsetseg "Ono" Anand, the recipient of
a large foundation grant for her prosthetic
clinic, visiting Washington, 2019.

As the time draws near to close my foundation, it looks as if we will end on a high note, having kick-started the renovation of Ono's impressive prosthetic clinic and provided it with the tools to grow. This facility and its staff will help the seriously disabled face their futures with hope and promise, not despair.

It has been a wonderful experience to establish a foundation to help others and most rewarding to work with dedicated people who give their hard-earned money and time for a cause they believe in. Indeed, it is overwhelming to think of the innate goodness of so many people, and I have regularly been touched by their generosity. Many of these are not wealthy at all, but they want to contribute and help.

I'm very proud to have been part of this world, even if only for a relatively brief time. I have come to admire my fellow Americans as being incredibly generous and helpful to others. All I can hope is that my daughters will find a way to create a family tradition of *non sibi*. I think they will, since already they are in "giving" professions—teaching and volunteering.

chapter 10

A Letter to
My Grandkids

November 9, 2016 *(the day after election day)*

Hi there, dear grandkids, Thomas, Andrew, Emily, and Abigail,

Your grandmother Mimsie has told me that you watched the election returns and are quite affected by them. I am so proud of you at your ages already taking interest in such important matters. Democracy succeeds only if an intelligent electorate thinks about such things and takes effective action. It may be as simple as voting, or as significant as making career choices.

In a democracy, all options are possible. Where there is a will, there is a way. You are learning that as you watch history unfold before your very eyes.

Andrew and Emily, your reactions were the ones reported most prominently, and so they aroused in me a most intense desire to take part in the discussion. I see myself in so much of what you worried about.

I understand you, Emily and Abigail, are concerned about your non-American friends who might be threatened with deportation. That is a sad thought, but best to stay optimistic. Governments move slowly and, given our history as a nation respecting human rights, things should end up okay. Believe me, most countries do not allow the freedoms we allow foreigners! Many nations are far more ruthless in kicking out foreigners when they feel like it. Your friends are fortunate to be here, and you always have the freedom to try to help them. They are lucky to have such caring and loving friends.

I'm proud of you all for speaking up. I always say, don't worry that people may criticize what you say; the important thing is to have said something at all. I didn't follow that principle when I was young; I was too timid to speak my mind until I was much older.

In Popsie's earlier days, the national stage in many ways reflected today's problems and reactions. It is important you understand this, because it might help you address our current challenges with a bit of detachment and a determination to "do your best and screw the rest," as the saying goes. This, too, shall pass.

We've had Trump-like events before. Actually, we've had many presidents who attracted negative attention, usually soon forgotten, and sometimes even amusing in retrospect. I remember the outrage when President Truman threatened to send a hamburger to a critic of Truman's daughter's musical talent. The meat was to be used for the black eye the critic was going to get from the president.

President Kennedy could get away with almost anything, even the shocking news that a woman's underpants were found under his pillow at the White

Left to right: Grandkids Andrew, Emily,
Abigail, and Thomas in Montana, June 2017.

House. More seriously, both presidents Nixon and
Clinton were faced with impeachment threats, Nixon
seriously enough to be forced to resign.

I was born during the Great Depression, which I
understand you, Andrew, are now studying. This was
the 1930s and 40s, and Franklin Delano Roosevelt was
president. I still remember vividly the atmosphere at
the time: outright hatred, particularly by the wealthy,
of FDR. New power to labor unions. High taxes.
Government intrusion into every facet of life.

American history until then was based on total free

enterprise, with large companies doing pretty much what they wanted. Cartels and monopolies flourished. Suddenly FDR threatened all that. Anti-trust laws were passed, and titans of industry like John D. Rockefeller and Andrew Carnegie were vilified. Obviously, this did not go over well with the upper class!

My personal memory is of my mother adoring FDR. I even pinned his photo on my wall. My dad, as a Swiss diplomat, was always very careful to stay out of political discussions. Obviously, mothers strongly influence their kids. I only focused on the less favorable things FDR did once I was in high school and college, learning of the Depression as a recent historical event.

Many people were horrified when FDR, upset that the Supreme Court blocked his more radical ideas, undertook to pack the court with three more members so that he would be guaranteed a majority. FDR eventually failed in his effort to change the Constitution, but he caused a lot of anguish.

If FDR had succeeded, we would probably be facing a very different world. Lesson to be learned? Democracy can be slow, but eventually it works. For us it has worked in fits and starts since 1789. As you may know, the US is one of the longest-surviving democratic nations in the world—quite an accomplishment.

FDR also wanted very much to enter the war against Nazi Germany. He looked at what was happening and was horrified. But we had many isolationists, even many who sympathized with the Nazis, who vehemently opposed our entry in the conflict. Only when the Japanese attacked Pearl Harbor did it become impossible to remain aloof. Still, for two years the Nazis were killing people, seizing countries, and we stood by.

Does it sound familiar? We are reluctant to engage in the war against Muslim extremists. They commit incredible atrocities while we watch. But getting involved in the conflict could also result in a disastrous entanglement in a war far from our shores. We'll see what happens, but I'm betting on our country. We'll work it out somehow.

When I was around your age, we were involved in a nasty and dangerous war in Korea. My classmates and I were constantly faced with the very real prospect that we could be drafted and sent off to fight in a war few of us understood.

Quite honestly, people used whatever means to legitimately postpone the draft. Most of us sought student deferments. As a result, while others less fortunate died, we lived peaceful lives as long as we went to school. Still, my parents were terrified that I might be suddenly drafted and sent to war.

It was my good fortune that the Korean War ended about the time I finished college. However, the draft remained, and one day I received my "Greetings, Ed Nef, you have been selected" (that is how draft letters began). My parents were crestfallen and had all sorts of ideas to exempt me from service, but I was smitten by a certain patriotism and said it was my duty to respond to the call. To this day, I remain rather pleased with myself for doing that.

The next two years I spent in the US Army. I was fortunate that my assignments were not too strenuous; the Korean War was over, and Vietnam was in its infancy. Still, two years spent on everything from field maneuvers to kitchen duty seemed like a terrible waste of my time. Rarely did the Cold War, which had started in earnest and was like a cloud over us all the time, intrude.

Not too many years later, I ended up at the opposite end of the foreign policy spectrum in the Peace Corps, the agency President Kennedy created in 1960 to promote cross-cultural understanding. JFK was an icon, a representative of the "new" America: full of life, vigor, and new ideas, not looking backward, but forward.

A can-do spirit filled the air, and the very idea that youth could serve their country to make the world a better place excited almost everyone. The Peace Corps personified that spirit, and JFK received full credit for coming up with such ideas. It was the first time youth were called to help people living in disadvantaged parts of the world.

I remember even today, I was working at my desk when Mimsie telephoned to say the radio had just announced Kennedy was shot. I couldn't believe it and rushed to the secretarial offices to find out if it were true. Peace Corps Director Sargent Shriver (who happened to be the brother-in-law of President Kennedy) was already behind closed doors with his wife and young son Timothy, who just happened to be stopping by.

A few minutes later, I remember the shock that went through the room when the White House called to tell Shriver the president was dead.

I watched as Timothy was rushed home and the door closed on Shriver's office. Shortly thereafter, a limousine came from the White House to take Shriver and his wife, Eunice, over there. Everyone at the Peace Corps was absolutely stunned. Work ceased as people gathered in small groups. Soon people started to drift home. As I recall, the offices were officially closed around 3:30 p.m. The rest of the afternoon was spent in front of the television.

Sunday evening, Mimsie and I decided to see the catafalque even though the news was discouraging about how many people were waiting to get in. We drove down to the capitol, where it seemed that hundreds of thousands of people had gathered. We got in line, but when we learned it was thirty blocks long and that we would not get in before it closed the following morning, we reluctantly gave up and headed home.

I remember going down to the National Cathedral the day after. I stood there for a couple of hours to see the funeral entourage come in and go out. There were thousands of people lining the streets, but I remember being overwhelmed by the silence that prevailed. One could almost hear a pin drop despite the hordes of people. Then I came home and watched the funeral on TV.

Over the next several days, there was a slow return to routine, although the routine as it existed was irremediably broken. The atmosphere was never again the same.

My parents—your great-grandparents—were hoarders and savers who boxed up letters from the family to be saved for posterity. As I go through these piles in occasional housekeeping moments, a letter catches my eye. I am grateful for the unusual insight occasionally imparted by some long-gone ancestor or relative.

I must admit, there are an awful lot of boring letters. My sister was great at reporting every time she washed her hair. But every now and then, a letter pops out of the mass and makes me grateful for the era of the hand-written letter and for my parents' inability to throw stuff away.

I came across a letter that I wrote to my parents on November 26, 1963, four days after JFK's assassination. It sent a feeling of sadness through me. What a great blow that assassination was for everyone. The letter reported to my parents the emotions, the shock, the confusion felt by all.

The tragic weekend has passed, and I still find I can't really believe it. It is difficult to try to describe the events of the last few days—everyone here was so stunned, shocked, and depressed. The New Frontier is gone, and although everyone criticized it or made fun of it, everyone here was inevitably a little bit part of it. Slowly the crowd will start to leave, and slowly, Harvardians will be replaced by Texans (this probably hurts as much as anything). The youth will be replaced by older people. The fun and the zest and (as everyone says) the style will be gone. Bobby Kennedy suddenly becomes "just" an attorney general. Shriver is just the head of another government agency. And the government drones on.

Also, all the names will start to disappear. Jackie's parties—always a tonic in the newspaper—will not be around anymore. Ted Sorensen apparently told Shriver today that although he plans to stay on for a while, he will leave soon. As he described it, after eleven years of working, writing and serving Kennedy, he just could not suddenly change and try to do the same for a new man. No matter how good.

I must say all this helps make Washington one of the most fascinating places to work. But it also makes it a sad place, a place where something like the events of the weekend inevitably affect everyone in a personal way. I suppose working for the Peace Corps makes one particularly feel this way. For nothing was more New Frontierish than the Peace Corps.

In re-reading this and other letters, I am struck by the "anti-Texas" undercurrent to my words. My deepest apologies to my friends from Texas. I report the comments only because I think they do reflect some of the conflict and perceptions one encountered in DC at the time.

Lyndon Johnson was seen almost as a usurper by

the old guard, and the tensions between Vice President Johnson and the president's supporters had been easily observed. Maybe it was simply the great disparity in backgrounds—Boston Brahmin versus Texas hard-knocks. It was also the fact that Johnson made his mark in the rough-and-tumble, wheeling and dealing of local politics, whereas JFK seemed to have been born into the upper levels of politics.

Having gone to Harvard and being younger than JFK, I was on the JFK side of the competition. In retrospect, LBJ handled an extremely tense and sensitive moment with great compassion and understanding. I'm not sure the Harvards ever gave him the credit he was due; they certainly didn't make it easy for him.

Although a life-long Democrat and a fan of JFK, I felt a certain kinship with President George H.W. Bush, who served thirty years after Kennedy, during the early 90s. A fellow Andover grad and an avid sailor, he was also known to have a fine sense of humor. On a whim, I wrote him a letter while he was president.

I was in a happy mood when I wrote that letter; after sending it, I did wonder about his reaction. But my instincts were correct. He had a wonderful sense of humor and maintained a camaraderie with schoolmates, no matter the difference in ages (he graduated from Andover in 1942, and I in 1951).

I admired him at the time I wrote the letter and was proud to have gone to the same school. I admired him even more when he obviously took my letter with the same good humor in which it was written. Forever after, I have held him in the highest regard: bright, even-tempered, fair and considerate, and a true gentleman.

Few people, in my opinion, were better prepared for the role of president than the first George Bush. A brave patriot, at age 18 he entered World War II as

November 14, 1991

The President
The White House
1600 Penna. Ave. NW
Washington, D.C.

Dear Mr. President,

It's uncanny.

You went to Andover. I went to Andover.

You're a natural born athlete. I'm a natural born athlete.

Upon retirement, you wish to sail the seven seas, and I have had the
same longing for several years.

Any interest in sharing expenses? We could shoot for a shakedown cruise
in the Spring of 1997, destination Thomas Point Lighthouse. If we get
that far without bickering, we can swing the old prow seaward to
adventure...

Of course, you will understand that since I went to Harvard, the
captaincy of the vessel has to stay with me. We could split lunch
preparation responsibilities. I genuinely believe Barbara and Liz (my
wife) would thoroughly enjoy such a cruise on a well managed boat.

I'm excited already. So do let me know your thoughts so that leisurely
preparations may begin.

Sincerely,

Edward Nef
Director

P.S. If you are still not a Redskins fan by then, the deal is off.

The letter I wrote to President Bush
in a light-hearted moment.

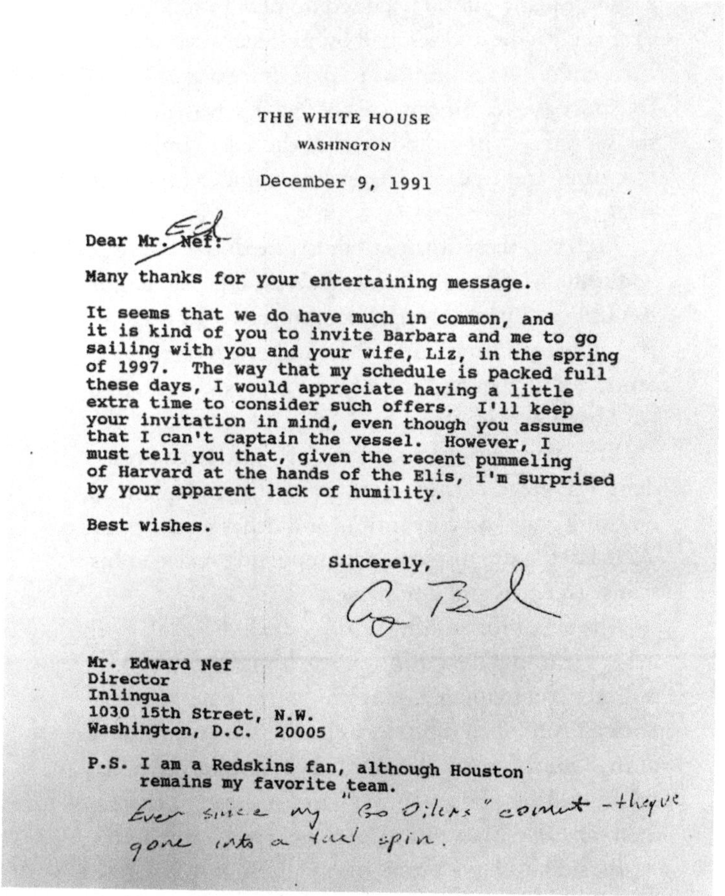

THE WHITE HOUSE

WASHINGTON

December 9, 1991

Dear Mr. ~~Nef~~ Ed:

Many thanks for your entertaining message.

It seems that we do have much in common, and
it is kind of you to invite Barbara and me to go
sailing with you and your wife, Liz, in the spring
of 1997. The way that my schedule is packed full
these days, I would appreciate having a little
extra time to consider such offers. I'll keep
your invitation in mind, even though you assume
that I can't captain the vessel. However, I
must tell you that, given the recent pummeling
of Harvard at the hands of the Elis, I'm surprised
by your apparent lack of humility.

Best wishes.

Sincerely,

George Bush

Mr. Edward Nef
Director
Inlingua
1030 15th Street, N.W.
Washington, D.C. 20005

P.S. I am a Redskins fan, although Houston
remains my favorite team.
Ever since my "Go Oilers" comment -they've
gone into a tail spin.

President Bush's good-natured
response to my letter.

a fighter plane pilot. He ended up being shot down over the Pacific and rescued by a US naval vessel. Incidentally, he continued to parachute out of planes for sport at over ninety years of age. He was elected to the Congress, appointed head of the CIA, ambassador to China, and elected vice president under President Reagan.

I tell you these stories to illustrate that we have had some wonderful presidents, both Democrat and Republican, most through election, a few by tragedy. A couple have been impeached and one has resigned. Some, on further and subsequent analysis, seemed to have been unfairly criticized.

President Ulysses S. Grant, our eighteenth president, was greatly criticized for favoritism, alcoholism, ignoring graft and corruption, and other weaknesses. Years later, more dispassionate reporting revealed his many strengths and kindnesses.

His talent for administration, flexibility, and openness to learning new things made him a successful military commander. Grant was an early supporter of African American rights as well as amnesty for leaders of the Confederacy. He handled economic and political crises deftly. His memoir, written shortly before he died, revealed his humility and great sense of humor.

President Harry Truman was also highly criticized. People made fun of his background as a haberdasher. Yet as time passed, he was given great credit for guiding us through the post-WWII difficulties and the start of the Cold War.

While it may be difficult to imagine now, a longer view of history can change how you think about things. As someone who has achieved a long view of most of my life, you'll have to take my word for it!

While I was in the Army, I thought I hated every minute of it, and I couldn't wait to get out. But the

longer I was out of the service, the more I looked back
on those two years as some of the most important
of my life. I "grew up" in the Army and got to know
Americans from all walks of life and all social strata.
We lived, ate, slept, worked, and grumbled together,
and those experiences made me appreciate our country
and the people who inhabit it.

I would advise you to take some time making up
your mind about the major detours and upsets in your
life. My Army service was an experience I now cherish;
I feel sorry for those who never had it. I am particularly grateful to my parents; they always let me make my
own final decisions and supported me no matter what.
What a blessing.

Life is a matter of ups and downs. Never let the
downs prevail. Keep up hope and go forward; things
inevitably will change. The circumstances of life—your
job, your president, the place you live—may not be
ideal, but an optimistic outlook can get you through
the worst of it.

It was reported that one of President George H.W.
Bush's guiding principles was simply, "Be kind." Think
how much better the world would be if we all remembered and obeyed those two words.

Just today by happenstance I was walking down
the sidewalk and passed the entrance to a retirement
home. Many were standing in front of it, looking
thoughtful or bored. As I walked by, I couldn't help
but flash them a smile and say something to the effect
that it looked like a neat meeting.

Several looked up, perhaps a bit surprised. When
they saw the comment was made in a friendly and kind
way, they too broke out in big smiles and made jocular
comments. It struck me how a kind smile and a cheerful comment elicited an equal response. Be kind. It
can't hurt, and it might make someone smile.

I'd really be happy if anyone remembered me for being kind. What a contribution, tiny as it might be, to one moment in a person's life. Being kind has the real possibility of making someone's day. You might catch them with a kindly comment at a moment when they feel down, and it could lift their spirits for the day.

Remember the proverb "Life is good, life is fair— and pretty cool, too." Actually, I just made that up.

Love you *lots* and *lots*!

Your cool Popsie

Grandson Thomas and me kayaking in Alaska.

Acknowledgements

I would like to thank:

+ Most of all, my ever-patient and always wise and helpful editor, Jane Constantineau

+ Family members Liz Nef, Christine Nef, Patricia Nef, and Stefanie Marik, who read all or parts of my manuscript

+ My loving parents, Victor and Maria Nef

+ My sister, Irene, and her daughter, Nancy, who both left us too early in their lives but whose presence and love I still feel

+ Meiyue Zhou, my longtime and trusted executive director of my foundation, who corrects my mistakes and makes great suggestions on how to proceed on just about anything

+ Damon Chung, whose technical expertise makes all our work possible, and his wife, MK, who brings good cheer and a sunny disposition to our work

+ My Swiss cousins Robert Nef, Barbara Scheiweiler, Erika Kuster, and Maja Nef, who made sure I was being accurate when mentioning Swiss ancestors

+ Mike Dow, who reminded me of the good times we had as GIs in Germany

+ Sue Firkins, my loyal niece, who reminded me of the good times we had at family reunions and elsewhere

+ Skip Cornelius, my late niece's husband, who was always around and ready to help whenever needed

+ Very patient and kind beta readers: my cousin, Alice Horn; ex-Army buddy who served with me in Germany, Paul Doherty; and old friend and former tennis partner, George Proctor

Films

Listed below are the films I produced with Santis Productions, LLC, my film company, now affiliated with my non-profit, The Ed Nef Foundation. They can be viewed at www.santisfilms.com.

Vietnam: The Reconciliation (2008)
US and Vietnamese people reconcile three decades after the war.

Polo: For the Love of Elephants (2009)
The story of the popular Asian sport of elephant polo and the conservation of elephants.

Mongolia: Mining Challenges a Civilization (2011)
The enormous impact caused by the mining industry. Available in two versions, Mongolian and English.

Mongolian/Tsaatan Bagel (2014)
How the Mongolian nomads bake their version of a bagel.

The Tsaatan—Revival of a Forgotten
Culture and Language (2014)
The Mongolian struggle to preserve culture and language.

Mongolian Mask Maker (2014)
How a Mongolian artist produces a facial mask.

Senegal Traveloque (2014)
The beauty of Senegal.

Senegalese Woman: A Challenge to Strife (2015)
How women keep Senegal a land of peace and promote
women's rights. Available in English and French versions.

Andover Class of '51–65th Reunion (2016)
A typical high school class reunion.

WWI: An American Martyr (2018)
The story of one of the first Americans to be killed in WWI.

Prosthetics: New Hope for Mongolian Amputees (2019)
The efforts of The Ed Nef Foundation to provide Mongolia
with a modern prosthetic facility.

About the Author

Born in New York City to a Swiss diplomat father and Polish mother, Ed Nef grew up immersed in multiple languages and cultures. After a two-year detour to Stuttgart, Germany, with the US Army, Ed entered the US Foreign Service in 1959.

Starting in Dakar, Senegal, as an economic officer, his assignments took him to Guatemala, Colombia, and Canada. Breaking up his State Department tours were two stints with the new US Peace Corps. In 1976, Ed won a State Department Congressional Fellowship to work on Capitol Hill, which led to a permanent position as legislative director for Senator Max Baucus of Montana.

A career in the rigid and bureaucratic State Department and years in the hectic world of politics left Ed wanting to create something of his own. He found a promising opportunity in the "businesses for sale" section of *The Washington Post*: a foreign language school. Ed bought the school and turned it into the largest independent private language-school in the Washington, DC area. Eventually, Ed opened English language schools in Tokyo, Mongolia, and Vietnam.

His fascination with the countries he visited—and a knack for the visual arts—led him into the world of documentary film production. He produced films on topics ranging from the post-war relationship between the US and Vietnam to the rights of women in Senegal and the mining industry in Mongolia.

In one last great adventure, Ed began a family foundation, The Ed Nef Foundation, to support worthy projects around the world. His latest effort is providing prosthetics to seriously disabled Mongolian individuals.

In the midst of his eclectic professional life, Ed managed to squeeze in another half a career as a flight instructor. Today, he lives with his wife, Elizabeth, in Northern Virginia. They have three daughters and four grandchildren.

Ed will be publishing an e-book and an audiobook under the same title.

Visiting Tsaatan reindeer people in northeast Mongolia near the Siberian border.